I DO

A BIBLE STUDY TO
DISCOVER YOUR POWER
PROTECT WHAT MATTERS
AND STOP FEELING
BAD ABOUT IT

BOUND

DARIES

BY HAVILAH CUNNINGTON

TABLE OF CONTENTS

ABOUT THE AUTHOR

I always knew God had a plan for other's lives, but never felt God could use me. I struggled with learning disabilities throughout my school years, which always caused me to have great insecurity about my value and worth.

It wasn't until the age of 17, as I was sitting in a car with friends on my way to a party, when I heard the voice of God speak to my heart, "There is more to life than this! I have called you. Come follow me." I spoke out that moment, telling those in the car that I had a call on my life and they were welcome to come with me, but I was going to serve God. I remember walking into my dark house, kneeling by my bed, and saying these simple words, "God, I'm not much. I'm young, I'm a girl with no special gifting, but if You can use anyone, You can use me."

Now, thinking back to that day, it makes me laugh how I'd hoped the heavens would have opened up, with angels descending and ascending on a heavenly ladder. It didn't happen. But I didn't need it. God heard my cry and was at work to accomplish His perfect will in my life.

By 19, my twin sister Deborah and I were traveling all over California preaching, teaching, and leading worship at any place that would have us. By 21, we had been in seven different states and Mexico teaching about Jesus and His great plan for this generation.

Now at 43, I've been in full-time ministry for 25 years. In 2016, my husband Ben and I started Truth to Table Ministries, and travel throughout the year speaking at conferences, churches, and events. During the week, we are passionate about helping purpose minded women live meaningful lives. We do this by creating online Bible studies, empowerment courses and lifestyle leadership resources for our Table Tribe members and the church at large.

We also have four young sons, Judah, Hudson, Grayson and Beckham, whom we love raising...along with our goldendoodle; Bear. If we're not traveling, our days are filled with bike rides, lake days and soccer games. It's a wild ride!

I believe today is the Church's finest hour, if we choose to live with passion, purpose and walk in power. I'm passionate about seeing individuals encountering God in a real way and seek to blow the lid off common misconceptions, personal limitations, and powerless living so others can become who God has designed them to be.

Havilah

For more resources please visit havilahcunnington.com & truthtotable.com

YOUR **GETTING** **STARTED** CHECKLIST

+ Your favorite pen & highlighter. Who doesn't love to track all the good finds while reading?

+ A fresh journal; something you can dream in.

+ Your Bible; choose what works best for you. The book Grasping God's Word breaks it down like this:

MORE FORMAL   **MORE FUNCTIONAL**

KJV	NASB	RSV	NRSV	NAB	NIV	NJB	NCV	GNB		THE MESSAGE
ASV	NKJV	HCSB	NET		TNIV	REB	NLT	CEB		THE PASSION
	ESV									AMP

In this study I reference both the NIV, TPT, The Message, and Amplified version.

+ Now grab your journal and write down 3 dreams; you have permission to dream!

+ Love all things Truth... join our Free Online Community: facebook.com/groups/truthtotable. You can also follow the study with live videos in addition to more resources by joining our global Truth to Table community. You can also get access to a full library of resources by becoming a member here: truthtotable.com/academy

WEEK ONE

OWNERSHIP

"I AM POWERFUL"

Welcome to Week One!

I'm thrilled you've decided to embark on the I DO BOUNDARIES study with me! During the next 15 days, we will unpack the truth about finding our personal power and protecting what matters.

Week One is all about finding your power through the influence of ownership.

We'll discover how boundaries operate, why God created them, and who is responsible for "what" in my life.

Let's get started!

DAY ONE

WHY AM I SO TIRED?

I WAS POWERLESS.

I'll never forget the day I abandoned my newborn son.

I arrived at church early that day to prepare for our three Sunday services. Juggling being a Worship Pastor and a new mom (*and wife*) in thirteen short months was, let's just say, complicated. I was excited to be back in the saddle, finally doing something I knew I could do well.

I didn't know how to be a mom, but I had years of leading worship, managing teams, and navigating services. Sure, there was no manual in the beginning years, but I'd forged my gifts and skills. I felt confident in my role.

I settled in as I took the lead that day. Things felt comfortable, familiar, and predictable. I took a deep internal breath and affirmed myself. *"Havilah, you can do this ... you can really do this."*

We were halfway through our worship practice when my newborn son, Judah, began to cry. It was distracting, so I signaled one of my girlfriends, asking for help. I held the microphone in one hand while signaling with the other that she could pick him up out of his car seat. *(Note: this was when it was ok to leave babies in their car seats.)*

I felt comfortable at this moment.

Not only could I see my friend, but I knew her well. If nothing else, her being a mom seemed to pre-qualify her... *right?* I continued to sing.

While rehearsing the third song, I watched my friend, still holding my firstborn, get up to walk towards the back of the room to greet her dad.

I turned to signal the team to transition. As I spun to the front to get my eyes back on my son, I noticed she wasn't holding him anymore. My eyes darted around the room, quickly seeing that she had passed Judah to her dad. I still had a flush of fear even though I casually knew her dad for a couple of years. My mind immediately interrupted, *"You have nothing to be concerned about; he's a grandpa; he's capable."*

But as she handed my newborn son to him and I watched him walk out the back doors of the auditorium, my brain said, *"He's just taking him to greet people."* Yet my inner gut said, *"You don't know him that well. GO GET YOUR BABY!"*

Immediately, I felt a sinking feeling.

My inner alarm was going off. I couldn't see my child. I didn't know where he was, and this never happened in his short eight weeks of life.

My brain promptly jumped to challenge my instincts. *"You can't just stop what you're doing. You have a whole room of adults depending on you. Many of them got up early, took care of their own children, and are here to practice. They've sacrificed to be here. It's not just about you. Don't be selfish."*

My thoughts continued.

"If you interrupt this moment, everyone will be waiting for you and they will probably think 'she's a new mom (insert eye roll) and she thinks she can do it all but, clearly, she's out of control. She's wasting all of our time.'"

I wanted to run off the stage through the back doors into the lobby and scoop my newborn son into my arms.

I stood there helpless... or at least that's how I felt.

I didn't know what to do. *So, you know what I did?*

I did NOTHING. Not a single thing.

I kept singing, mic in hand, with the team following my cues, even though I couldn't see my son. His car seat sat empty.

And I stood there. Paralyzed.

I didn't know what to do. My world was colliding, and I was speechless and powerless.

A few minutes later, the dad walked back into the room with my son in his arms. He handed him back to his daughter as she happily placed him back in his car seat, pulling the blanket around his sleeping body.

The day continued. I never told anybody. *"How could I have done nothing?"*

I felt humiliated. Ashamed.

On the way home, tears filled my eyes as I rehearsed the circumstances.

I couldn't even muster up the courage to tell my husband Ben what I had done. Quickly pushing away the feelings of disgrace, I told myself it wouldn't happen again and, for a little while, that was true.

But time would tell the truth.

I was powerless in an internal war.

UNDERSTANDING THE WAR WITHIN

The battle between "who I NEED to be" and "who I AM" raged deep inside.

I DIDN'T KNOW HOW I COULD DO THE <u>RIGHT THING</u> AND KEEP EVERYONE HAPPY WHEN THE <u>RIGHT THING</u> WASN'T WHAT EVERYONE WANTED.

How could I keep everyone happy without doing what they needed or wanted me to do? How DO I do the right thing above ALL things when I needed to be the girl everyone thought I was?

I wish I could say this didn't happen again, but I watched myself make these types of decisions for years. Of course, I got better at damage control. I could anticipate it going poorly and do my best to protect what mattered to me, yet there were moments, and I mean precise, evident moments, where I chose what people thought of me over what I knew was best. Frankly, it was collateral damage.

However, this didn't just start when I became a wife or a new mom. These internal narratives were formed when I was a child. Let me explain:

INTERNAL NARRATIVES

People's opinions of me hung in the balance of my behavior. I was that powerful!

If people were happy with me, then I was doing something right. If they were upset, I was doing something wrong. It was that simple. The internal narrative sounded like, *"Other's approval of you helps you know how you're doing overall. It also helps you know how God may be feeling about you as well."* It was never that blunt, but very much communicated. I thought, *"God holds me responsible for other's thoughts and feelings."*

If I hurt someone, I should be a good girl and make it right. I was responsible for how they felt about me.

If I acknowledged and apologized for my wrongs (*even bringing myself to tears to show my remorse*), then they would forgive me immediately or at least eventually. After all, I was that powerful, right? My response could trigger a good or poor response. I was completely responsible for others. In fact, how others saw me could hurt how they saw God. I single-handedly held God's reputation in my hands.

These beliefs sounded good. While I was young, energetic, and flexible, I didn't have a problem with them because they served me well. These beliefs made me feel in control and powerful.

I COULDN'T PLEASE EVERYONE

The real conflict showed up when I became a mom. **I couldn't please everyone at the same time.** There weren't enough hours in a day, and my human capacity was tapped out.

BEING NICE OUT OF FEAR WASN'T WORKING.

My power over others' feelings and beliefs kept me running around, trying to *"do the right thing."* My reality and theology were colliding. Working harder wasn't working, and taking responsibility for others was slowly killing me.

IF WHAT I BELIEVED WAS TRUE, THEN WHY WAS I SO OVERWHELMED, ANXIOUS, AND FEELING LIKE I WAS CONTINUALLY LETTING OTHERS DOWN? WHY WAS I WORKING SO HARD?

I want us to read the words of Matthew.

"Come to Me, all who are weary and heavily burdened [by religious rituals that provide no peace], and I will give you rest [refreshing your souls with salvation]. 29 Take My yoke upon you and learn from Me [following Me as My disciple], for I am gentle and humble in heart, and you will find rest (renewal, blessed quiet) for your souls. 30 For My yoke is easy [to bear] and My burden is light." Matthew 11:28-30 (AMP)

Let's read this part again. **"My yoke is easy, my burden is light."**

I wasn't feeling an easy yoke, and I sure wasn't carrying a light burden. The more I served Him, the more responsibility He gave me. And, in turn, the more responsibility He gave me, the more I felt like I was disappointing Him.

Have you experienced similar feelings?

Ones that are the exact opposite to the verse above?

Heavy burdens and unbearable yokes? Burn out, exhaustion, and fatigue from serving? Yeah. Me too.

What I'm about to say will put things into perspective and I want you to think hard about it:

GOD DOESN'T HAVE TO ABUSE ME TO USE ME.

Do you and I believe this? If so, then maybe, just maybe, we are putting more responsibility on ourselves than God ever intended. If His yoke becomes easy and His burden light, couldn't we conclude we are going in the right direction? Maybe we've confused responsibility and ownership.

I have found the road leading out of this predicament. There is a way, but it's going to take some rewiring of our internal hard drives. We have to change in order for things to change. Period.

GOD DOESN'T HAVE TO ABUSE ME TO USE ME.

REME MBER

+ I will face battles between "who I NEED to be" and "who I AM" currently.

+ Being nice out of fear doesn't work.

+ When my reality and theology collide, it's time to lean in and learn.

+ Working harder doesn't work.

+ Taking responsibility for others doesn't work.

+ *God says, "My yoke is easy, my burden is light."*

+ God doesn't have to abuse me to use me.

LET'S ACTIVATE THIS STUFF IN OUR LIVES!

"Are you tired? Worn out? Burned out on religion? Come to me. Get away with me and you'll recover your life. I'll show you how to take a real rest. Walk with me and work with me—watch how I do it. Learn the unforced rhythms of grace. I won't lay anything heavy or ill-fitting on you. Keep company with me and you'll learn to live freely and lightly."
Matthew 11:28-30 (Message Version)

All spiritual growth comes from God and it's only possible with His help. I love how this is paraphrased in the Message version: "Walk with me and work with me—watch how I do it."

Three things will happen as I invest in this study.

1. Walk - I Will Walk with God

I will learn what it looks like to walk and talk with God. Our core theology (the study of God) is grounded in having a relationship with Him. Healthy relationships require communication and a significant amount of time together. My relationship with God will need both of those things to thrive.

2. Work - I Will Work with God

There's going to be things God asks me to do, and I will immediately know how to do it. Other things I won't know how to do or where to start. Both are ok as long as I purpose to walk with God. Living for

God will take my full determination. There are no shortcuts. I will have to do the work. Period.

3. Watch - We Will Watch Him Do It

The first two steps are within my responsibility. But this last step is to acknowledge what God can and will do for me. This study is designed to help me see God at work in my everyday life.

RESPOND

"For this very reason, adding your diligence [to the divine promises], employ every effort in exercising your faith to develop virtue (excellence, resolution, Christian energy), and in [exercising] virtue [develop] knowledge (intelligence), ..." 2 Peter 1:5 Amplified

I love how Peter puts it! We are to add diligence to God's divine promises. It will take every effort to exercise our faith. Why? Because it helps us increase our resolution to be free! It will cause our energy and virtue to grow. I love this point!

Diligence is a God idea! Hard work is something that He divinely orchestrated to help us get where we need to go. To build a life that protects that which matters most is going to require me to be diligent. More diligent than I've ever had to be before. I may not have been trained for this, but I was made for it. If I give it my full attention, I'm promised a breakthrough.

Our final stop today is to make a commitment to ourselves. A promise that I am going to follow through with this three-week journey. I may not have heard this before, but each time I make a commitment to myself and follow through on that commitment, I build trust with myself. Trust builds *confidence*. The opposite is true, too. When I don't follow through with what I've told myself, trust is broken. It leads to *insecurity*.

On the next page is a *Spiritual Life Contract*. Take a moment before signing it. Think about what it's going to take and the sacrifice you will need to make for the next couple of weeks to follow through. Count the cost.

Once you've signed it, put it somewhere you can see it. Rip it out and post it on your bathroom mirror, your office cubicle, or anywhere you'll see it on a daily basis. I promise you will have a ton more confidence, just following through with this commitment.

MY SPIRITUAL
JOURNEY CONTRACT

I, _____,

declare I must lead in every area of my life. I will no longer settle for living a life less than what I know God's called me to live. I have had enough experiences living less than my best. I know it's my TIME TO CHANGE. God has set me up for success.

I will dedicate myself to enrich the quality of my life from what it is right now. I will persevere under any circumstance to act upon the healthy mindsets outlined in this book, which are going to empower me. I will not leave any healthy perspective unlearned, and will relentlessly work to empower my life and push beyond my known limits into God's marvelous provision.

I AM responsible for shaping my destiny and entrust my ability to see this book through. I understand that the only way to real success is by having an excellent state of mind, and I'm willing to vigorously work to create and enhance it. I am ready to LOVE MY LIFE in the never-ending journey of self-growth, using the unlimited power of the Holy Spirit.

I am ready to attain a burning desire, compelling vision, and a passion for life that only God can provide.

Sign: _____

Date: _____

WHAT'S THE BIG DEAL ABOUT BOUND -ARIES?

Proverbs 25:28 says, *"Like a city whose walls are broken down is a man who lacks self-control."*

I've been a Christian for a long time and I know what I believe. On top of that, I was raised by a ministry family and, eventually, created one myself. I've heard thousands of messages, taken Bible classes, attended ministry schools, and listened to hundreds of biblical podcasts. You get the picture. But what I'm about to say, I'm a little embarrassed to admit: *I had never heard one sermon on this certain subject and didn't know anything about it until just a few years ago.*

It wasn't until I was in the middle of postpartum depression and my life was falling apart, that a female Christian counselor began to break this down for me. As she shared, it was almost like I was listening to a foreign language. I had no idea what she was talking about, but was captivated with the subject.

I always knew being a Christian had some fundamental precepts. Specifically, the first two of the Ten Commandments:

1. There should be no other gods before you.

2. You should love your neighbor as yourself.

I'd never stopped to ask myself what it would look like to love "me" well. After all, I tried hard to love who God made me be, and that seemed to be enough. Didn't that encompass all that self-acceptance was intended to be?

It wasn't until my life began to fall apart while doing all the right things for all the right reasons, that I began to ask myself some serious questions.

What didn't I know? What am I missing?

Let's start at the beginning.

WHAT IS A GODLY BOUNDARY?

Our world consists of boundaries. It's easy to see them all around us. We've built fences, signs, walls, and hedges. We've created cities, counties, states and countries. We use them to clarify ownership. These lines help us know who owns what and where. Once we know who the owner is, we know who is responsible. The owner of the property is legally responsible. The non-owner isn't.

As our physical world has boundaries, so, too, our spiritual world. They are harder to see, but just as important.

Boundaries don't just keep the good in, but also keep the bad out.

THEY KEEP US FROM HARM AND PROTECT SAFE AND HEALTHY LOVE.

My life is my property. As the owner of my life, I have specific property lines. **Property lines allow me to know where I am personally responsible. They show me where I have complete ownership.** Ownership requires responsibility. Without property lines, I don't know who is accountable for what and how to take care of my life in a healthy way.

Last year, we put a pool in our yard. After seven years of debilitating heat, the kind of heat that makes you want to lose your mind for four straight months every summer, we bit the bullet. Before we could break ground, the engineer came over and showed us his plans. *They were glorious!*

BOUNDARIES HELP US PROTECT WHAT MATTERS MOST TO US.

I could instantly see our four young, crazy boys jumping into our glistening pool. Our dream was finally growing legs. We signed papers and handed over the first check of many. The following week he came to the house to map out the pool. He used spray paint to create the footprint, outline the landscaping, and mark where the fence would land. *It was so exciting!*

As the engineer gathered his belongings to leave, he mentioned one last thing, *"I need to check out your property line to make sure we are good to go. I'll submit these plans to the city, and we should be able to break ground next week, give or take. Let's go find that property line!"* We jumped up from the table, walking out the front door, and towards the corner of the yard.

The engineer was quietly concentrating as we all stood there waiting. I asked him, *"How do you know where our property line is?"* I honestly had no idea. He explained, *"The city puts a little X on the side of the road. We can measure 20 feet from that X to build your pool."*

He'd found it! He pointed to a little sun-faded X. Apparently, there were marks like this at each corner of the owned property, or at least they were there in the beginning. Now that we'd found our property line, we could move forward. We knew what belonged to us and what belonged to the city.

I HAVE COMPLETE OWNERSHIP

Our lives are the same way. **God has given you and I complete ownership of our lives.** Each of the lines (built from our conclusions, beliefs, opinions, attitudes, past experiences, and social learning) defines where we begin and where someone else ends—a clear and present understanding of what belongs to whom. What's yours is yours, and what's mine is mine. Period.

We must understand this truth. It's so critical, God even put it in the very first chapter of the Bible.

> **God blessed them and said to them, "Be fruitful and increase in number; fill the earth and subdue it. Rule over the fish in the sea and the birds in the sky and over every living creature that moves on the ground."**
> **Genesis 1:28 - NIV**

God outlined from the beginning of time where Adam and Eve would have leadership and authority. He commanded them, "subdue" and "rule over" what I have given you. He wasn't confused about ownership and governance. He commanded it.

Note: This is before the fall of creation. Ruling and subduing isn't a cause of the Fall, but instead, it is in the heart of God to make us powerful people.

We understand ownership when authority is given to us. God knew that if He gave Adam and Eve ownership, they would walk in their rightful authority. You and I, too, are made in the image of God and created to take full ownership and responsibility for our lives. We please God when we take full ownership of our properties. Knowing the difference between what is mine and what is yours makes life manageable—even enjoyable.

> *"Any confusion of responsibility and ownership in our lives is a problem of boundaries"* 1 - Townsend & Cloud

---

1Boundaries Dr. Henry Cloud and Dr. John Townsend Page 27

BOUNDARIES ARE CRITICAL FOR HEALTHY RELATIONSHIPS. MY PRIMARY GOAL IN HAVING CLEAR BOUNDARIES IS TO PROTECT MY RELATIONSHIPS.

BOUNDARIES PROTECT MY RELATIONSHIP WITH MYSELF.

The first relationship is with me. When I have boundaries and internal limits, I know exactly where I begin and where I end. I trust myself. I trust myself to enforce my limitations. When I require ownership, I develop a healthy relationship with myself and with others. I believe what I say. I can communicate to others what they can and cannot do—with conviction. Doing this builds confidence. Confidence in myself. Boundaries will help you define and guard your soul (Proverbs 4:23). They save our lives!

BOUNDARIES PROTECT OUR RELATIONSHIPS WITH OTHERS.

When I know who is responsible for what, I can relax. I don't have to over-function, trying to be God in the lives of others' *(we will talk more about that tomorrow).* Or, I can swing the other way and under-function by not taking ownership and allowing others to take responsibility for areas God clearly entrusted to me. I don't have to be others-controlled but self-controlled. Whew!

WHEN WE CAN COMMUNICATE OUR BOUNDARIES, WE CAN LIVE WITHOUT FEAR OF

VIOLATION AND MORE WITHIN SACRIFICIAL LOVE.

Even seriously believing Christians have a tough time with boundaries. *I'm the first to raise my hand!* I was so confused. I began to see how my boundary issues could be linked to harmful areas in my life like anxiety, depression, misplaced guilt, and shame, which caused me enormous pain. I could also see how it was linked to many broken relationships and marital struggles. My eyes were opened!

I was desperate to learn.

Many of my struggles were solved by merely knowing WHO was responsible and by taking ownership of my personal property.

BOUNDARIES ALLOW ME TO KNOW THE ANSWERS TO LIFE'S TOUGHEST QUESTIONS: WHO IS THE OWNER AND WHO IS ULTIMATELY RESPONSIBLE?

REME MBER

+ A boundary is where I begin and others end.

+ A boundary is a place I have full ownership.

+ Boundaries allow me to feel safe.

+ Boundaries keep the good in and the bad out.

+ Owners are legally responsible for what happens on his or her property.

+ Non-owners are not responsible for other properties.

+ Boundaries make our lives manageable and enjoyable.

Like a city that is broken down and without walls [leaving it unprotected] is a man who has no self-control over his spirit [and sets himself up for trouble].
Proverbs 25:28 (AMP)

When we have no self-control, we are open to letting someone else take the ownership that was assigned to us from Heaven. Galatians tells us that the world, enemy, or even our own flesh rule over these kinds of people (Galatians 5:22-23). Think about it: a city without walls goes unprotected. The property lines are indistinguishable and anyone can now claim the land for themselves. When we have self-control, we have self-confidence. When we have self-confidence, we have the ability to set healthy boundaries, like a city with a fortress.

RESPOND

Think of your life as a city. Are there any broken down walls? Ask the Holy Spirit what happened to cause this.

_____

_____

_____

_____

_____

What does it look like to start rebuilding? What property lines need to be created?

_____

_____

_____

_____

Now, imagine your life as a city completely rebuilt with strong walls and a thriving life. What have you implemented to keep your city standing strong?

_____

_____

_____

_____

DOES GOD HAVE BOUND -ARIES TOO?

I couldn't believe I was invited.

I imagined this moment for years. I played it out in my daydreams. I even dreamt of our meeting in my sleep. What I would say. How I would act. I couldn't believe I was about to meet my real-life hero.

As the room filled up with other admirers, we sat there, anticipating her arrival. The room buzzed with excitement. *"This is really happening,"* I told myself. *"Deep breaths. Act normal."* But I was feeling far from normal. The door opened and there she was. My brain was quickly trying to catch up with all of the images I had created in my head.

"She looks a lot younger than I thought ... and prettier, much prettier." There was a powerful atmosphere around her and, with a smile, she greeted the room. On the other hand, we looked like a room full of pound puppies begging to make eye contact.

She sat in front with a few other leaders facing us. Watching her every move, we sat breathlessly waiting for the next moment.

The day continued as minutes turned to hours and hours to a full day. We listened, asked questions, and mustered up the courage to ask for a photo.

As I sat watching this female powerhouse, I knew my life would never be the same. I couldn't unsee what I witnessed. Don't get me wrong; she already had my attention and my admiration. But this was more than that.

I observed her strength.

I felt her fervor.

I studied her every move; her every answer.

One thing was obvious: she was extremely clear about her choices. She wasn't confused. She had a rock-solid "yes" and a rock-solid "no." Her direction was blatantly obvious. When she answered our questions, she never contradicted herself—never vacillating about her answer. She lived it out, and her "yes" and "no" guarded her very being. These answers were the force behind her powerful life.

She had a "yes" about her bedtime. A "no" about what she was willing to eat. She knew what she liked to wear and only wore those items. She had a "yes" about how she traveled, and multiple "no's" to protect her energy. Everything choreographed—all choices directed towards a purpose.

As I sat there, learning, listening, and absorbing every morsel of information, I was amazed. I didn't feel pressured to adopt her personal 'yes's' or 'no's.'

Instead, I left feeling a resolve to define my boundaries. I had permission. Permission to say "yes" to things I desperately wanted to and "no" to feeling bad if others didn't approve. I witnessed how seemingly insignificant decisions held enormous power—my "yes" and "no" held at bay my very purpose.

Today, we're going to look at why boundaries aren't just helpful but profoundly spiritual.

Boundaries are a popular topic. But make no mistake, property lines have been an idea from the very beginning.

GOD CREATED BOUNDARIES FOR THE SAKE OF ORDER, OWNERSHIP, AND PROTECTION.

BOUNDARIES AREN'T JUST HELPFUL BUT PROFOUNDLY SPIRITUAL.

He's very passionate about boundaries. He knows that when we have ownership, love is protected. When we allow love to motivate us, we can live whole lives by clearly knowing where we end and others begin. His Kingdom works!

God holds Himself to the same order, ownership, and protection.

"God defines himself as a distinct, separate being, and he is responsible for himself. He defines and takes responsibility for his personality by telling us what he thinks, feels, plans, allows, will not allow, likes, and dislikes."
- Townsend and Cloud

THE TRINITY

Let's look at the Holy Trinity for a moment.

We believe in our Heavenly Father, Jesus His Son, and the Holy Spirit.

"God exists as three persons, yet he is one being. Each person of the Trinity—the Father, Son, and Holy Spirit—has a separate identity while yet possessing the full nature of God." - John McDowell

Each person of the Godhead leads with distinct autonomy but perfect unity. Each also has a role, responsibility, and relationship. The Holy Spirit didn't die on the Cross; that was Jesus's role. Jesus didn't return to the Earth as the Comforter and Counselor but instead sent the Holy Spirit. Each person in the Godhead holds a position and ownership. Each respects the boundaries of the others.

GOD HAS BOUNDARIES

God demonstrates boundaries over and over again to us through scripture.

In the Book of Revelation, it says, **"I stand at the door and knock..."** *Revelation 3:20 (NKJV)* It continues, **"If you don't open it up, I'm coming in anyway because I'm all-knowing, all-powerful and a righteous God."**

No, it doesn't say that at all!

It continues, **"If anyone hears My voice and opens the door, I will come in to him and dine with him, and he with Me."** *Revelation 3:20 (NASB)* God, Who absolutely has the power to override our free will and do it anyway, holds Himself to boundaries, property lines, and ownership.

We see Him use perfect boundaries.

He stands at the door.

He knocks.

He calls out, using His words. He communicates what He wants but only continues to come in if invited. *WOW! Just take that in for a minute.* I can't help but think of the times I've tried to barge into others' lives by knocking down doors. All because I thought I knew what they needed. Insert eye roll. I thought I knew what was better for their life.

It's humbling to see God will never violate our boundaries when He knows what's best for us. He allows our free will to operate even when He knows the outcome may jeopardize our future. He respects our power of choice, our right for ownership, and our free will.

Why does God respect our boundaries?

Boundaries are in His nature.

Let's look at how God defines Himself through boundaries in Scripture.

It will open our eyes to see how boundaries protect us by keeping the good in and the bad out.

+ God communicates His boundary: *"I am loving."*

"And so we know and rely on the love God has for us. God is love. Whoever lives in love lives in God and God in them." *1 John 4:16 (NIV)*

We can immediately know that if it's not loving, it's not on His property. If it's full of hate, then it's outside of God's property line.

+ God communicates His boundary: *"I am light."*

"If we claim to have fellowship with him and yet walk in the darkness, we lie and do not live out the truth." *1 John 1:6 (NIV)*

+ God communicates His boundary: *"If you walk in darkness, you can't walk with Me."*

God communicates, *"I'm not responsible to get the darkness out of you. If you want Me to come in and kick the darkness out, I'll be happy to do that with you. I'm light. I hang out with light. If you hang around Me, you can expect the light to be valuable. My presence carries light. I'm the owner of light."*

REME MBER

+ Be clear, not confused, about your choices.

+ I don't need others to approve of my boundaries.

+ Boundaries are in God's nature.

+ God created boundaries for the sake of order, ownership, and protection.

+ Each person in the Godhead leads with distinct autonomy but perfect unity.

+ The Father, Son, and Holy Spirit respect the boundaries of each other.

+ God respects our power of choice, our right for ownership, and our free will.

Let's look at the life of Jesus; I want us to see a few things about how He lived.

1. Jesus Lived a Perfect Life

The Bible says, *"He committed no sin, and no deceit was found in his mouth."* 1 Peter 2:22 (NIV)

Jesus was without sin, which means He lived a perfect life. When we look at how Jesus lived, we can see how we should live. He gives us an ideal road map.

2. Jesus Dealt with the Same Stuff We Do

"For we do not have a High Priest who is unable to sympathize and understand our weaknesses and temptations, but One who has been tempted [knowing exactly how it feels to be human] in every respect as we are, yet without [committing any] sin." Hebrews 4:15 (AMP)

Jesus, knowing exactly how it feels to be human, shows us how to deal with the demands of life. As we study the life of Jesus, it's evident **He had a hard "yes" and a hard "no." He** never vacillated about who He was or what He was here to do. Jesus didn't ruminate on every decision, trying to please everyone. His "yes" was always moving Him toward His ultimate goal. His purpose was clear. Even when His "yes" would disappoint others, He didn't allow it to sidetrack Him.

RESPOND

To live a life of powerful boundaries, we need to kick people-pleasing to the curb. I had to be confident in my "yes" and "no" to do this and stick to it!

1. Define your "yes" and "no" — these are your non-negotiables. When it comes to your time, relationships, career choices, family choices, finances, etc., what is your "yes" and "no"?

_____

_____

_____

_____

_____

_____

_____

2. Keep your list of non-negotiables where you can review them often. Tell your spouse or a close friend what they are to keep yourself accountable!

3. Use your "no" this week! And then do it again. This will protect your "yes." It will probably feel uncomfortable, but comfort doesn't bring change. Your "no" is the key to freedom!

AM I ACTING LIKE A SPIRITUAL GROWN UP?

"Others can, but I cannot."

I heard this phrase a lot growing up. I didn't understand its spiritual value until I was much older. It holds an essential Godly principle which is talked about in the Bible in **1 Corinthians 10:23**. *I love the Amplified version!*

"All things are legitimate [permissible—and we are free to do anything we please], but not all things are helpful (expedient, profitable, and wholesome). All things are legitimate, but not all things are constructive [to character] and edifying [to spiritual life]."
1 Corinthians 10:23

I'M NOT CREATED TO DO ALL THINGS

Part of having **Godly boundaries is understanding you are not created to do all things. Doing all things will not be helpful to you.** There are a bunch of things you can do, but according to the Bible, they are not always beneficial.

What does that mean?

Your eternal destiny isn't in jeopardy if you choose to do or not do specific things. God won't stop you, but He knows it's not always His best for you. The good thing can still get in the way of the God thing.

PART OF BEING A SPIRITUAL GROWNUP IS UNDERSTANDING WHAT IS NOT ONLY PERMISSIBLE FOR ME, BUT WHAT IS ACTUALLY HELPFUL IN MY LIFE.

Instead of me thinking thoughts like, *"Do I have time for that?"* or *"Could I pull that off?"* I need to be asking questions like, *"What are the things that keep my life profitable and wholesome?"* or *"What actually helps me construct good character and edifies my spiritual life?"*

Let's off-ramp for a minute.

Did you know God sees you and me as spiritual grown-ups?

BECOMING A SPIRITUAL GROWN-UP

God doesn't count how many years you've been a Christian to see if you should be seen as a spiritual grown-up or not. If I'm an adult, then I'm an adult to God. He knows I hold power to make my own choices, choose my path, and respond with maturity. He holds me accountable for being an adult. We can often think that because we might be a baby Christian (new in our faith walk), God sees us as children. This is true for our spiritual growth, but not our ownership and responsibility. God holds me entirely responsible for my life. He knows it's possible for me to live an abundant life without anyone else participating.

MY BELIEFS, EMOTIONS, AND DECISIONS ALL BELONG TO ME. I CAN SEE THAT AS A BURDEN OR I CAN SEE IT AS A POSITION OF POWER.

Because God sees me as a spiritual adult, it's my responsibility to figure out what things are beneficial for me. It is also my job to figure out what is not helpful to me… *the things I can do, but shouldn't.*

When it comes to boundaries, only I, with the help of the Holy Spirit, will be able to set them in a healthy place. My life, time, and relationships are mine alone, and they require tailor-made boundaries and limits.

My personal boundaries and limits will not work in your life and vice versa. It is critical that we each cooperate with the Holy Spirit and God's Word in order to live healthy lives with clear boundaries.

Before I had children, my schedule was crazy. I had no problem staying up late, getting up early and jumping from one thing to another. But, as I started having kids, my life became more complicated. The invites don't stop even with a growing family. Often, it was a new mom's group, a birthday party, a Bible study, or serving in some area. I would get invited to something and instantly felt an enormous pressure to pull it off. Even when it was something I wanted to do, I didn't know how I could.

I would try to do it all, dragging my babies from event to event. I was always tired. My kids' meltdowns were often, as were their naps in car seats, and dinner was always some sort of drive-through meal. I lived with an anxiety that I would let someone down at any moment. If I did let someone down, which was inevitable, I didn't have enough margin to deal with the conflict. When this ever juggling lifestyle became difficult, I would tell myself, *"It's OK! I'm serving them and God is happy with me. I must be here. They would do the same for me."* I would talk myself down from the stress I was feeling.

I began to make better choices for myself, long term, when I realized that my life was completely under my own responsibility and ownership.

I was immature. I made immature decisions. My decisions were "me-focused" and circled a momentary feeling of joy, rather than a long term benefit from my choices. My choices were fueled by what felt good. It felt good to be the chief problem solver. It felt good to save the day. This type of thinking was immature and would eventually hurt me.

GOD WASN'T ASKING ME TO BE THE SAVIOR. HE'D ALREADY FILLED THAT POSITION.

How many of us would say we're *"living the abundant life, but we're exhausted, worn out, and unfulfilled?"* Could it be that we're the ones keeping us from the life Christ came to give us?

GETTING MY POWER BACK

I made healthier choices once I understood that God wasn't going to interrupt me from my own self-imposed *to-do list,* and that I had the ability to control my life and schedule by saying, "No." I got my power back! The power I had all along. I was a powerful spiritual adult!

TRUTH: WE CAN'T PROTECT WHAT MATTERS MOST IF WE'RE BUSY PROTECTING OUR REPUTATION.

When I started to view myself the way God saw me, a powerful spiritual adult, I knew things had to change. It was going to take a lot of work to undo the years of wrong thinking. Here's what a Godly leader told me in the face of radical transformation: "TAKE ALL THE TIME YOU NEED." There's no rush! God isn't going to leave you behind.
Lean in and let go of the timeline of growth. Embrace life, "moment-by-moment," and you'll find the path to abundant living. Life will get so much easier!

WE CAN'T PROTECT WHAT MATTERS MOST IF WE'RE BUSY PROTECTING OUR REPUTATION.

Imagine living a life full of powerful, intentional choices. Imagine what it will be like to know what's most important to you and creating an experience that protects that very thing. Most of all, imagine being able to communicate your priorities, live them out, and stop feeling bad about it!

REME MBER

+ Living with Godly boundaries is understanding I am not created to do all things.

+ Doing all things will not be beneficial to me.

+ God sees me as a spiritual grown-up.

+ God knows I can live an abundant life without anyone else participating.

+ My life, time, and relationships are mine alone, and they require tailor-made boundaries and limits.

+ God wasn't asking me to be the savior. He'd already filled that position.

+ I can't protect what matters most if I'm busy protecting my reputation.

+ In the face of radical transformation, TAKE ALL THE TIME YOU NEED.

"As a man thinks in his heart so is he."
Proverbs 23:7

The Bible says I will end up acting out in my choices by what I think of myself. My beliefs determine my behavior.

Think about this:

+ If I see myself as a loser, I'm going to lose a lot in life.

+ If I see myself as a victim, I'm going to let other people victimize me.

+ If I see myself as not creative, I'll never create anything.

+ If I see myself as a failure, I'm going to fail often.

+ What I see is what I get. Period.

If I've always seen myself as a little girl in a grown-up world, I will have a hard time showing up as an adult. My choices will mirror my immaturity. It's

going to take determination and discipline to begin to see me as God sees me.

Each time I start to feel powerless, I'm going to remind myself I have everything I need to succeed. Take a moment, meditate on this verse, and put it to memory.

I can do all things [which He has called me to do] through Him who strengthens and empowers me [to fulfill His purpose—I am self-sufficient in Christ's sufficiency; I am ready for anything and equal to anything through Him who infuses me with inner strength and confident peace.] Philippians 4:13

"A good man out of the good treasure of his heart brings forth good things, and an evil man out of the evil treasure brings forth evil things." Matthew 12:35

The way we think determines the way we act. What we believe will come out in our lifestyle. Our beliefs determine our behavior. Often we're acting on false or inaccurate information about ourselves.

RESPOND

Today, I declare: I am leaving my childish ways behind me so I can fully live as my adult self. I intentionally choose to protect what matters most to me, despite what disappointment it may bring to others. Jesus has given me the authority to live a powerful life.

THINGS I'M LEAVING IN CHILDHOOD

_____

_____

_____

_____

_____

THINGS I'M BRINGING INTO ADULTHOOD

_____

_____

_____

_____

_____

AM I DOING TOO MUCH FOR TOO MANY PEOPLE?

If you get a chance, turn to **Galatians 6:2-5** in your Bible and read.

> **Carry each other's burdens, and in this way you will fulfill the law of Christ. If anyone thinks they are something when they are not, they deceive themselves. Each one should test their own actions. Then they can take pride in themselves alone, without comparing themselves to someone else, for each one should carry their own load.** Galatians 6:2-5 (NIV)

Paul clearly outlines boundaries, limits, and property lines that we should be operating within this passage. He is writing a letter to the Church, explaining how we should live out our faith.

WHAT ARE BURDENS?

His first words, *"Carry each other's burdens,"* speaks loudly of our spiritual mandate. The word **burden** comes from the Greek word *baros,* meaning *an excessive and crushing load*. It gives us a picture of a huge boulder. The image portrays someone who is carrying a burden so heavy, they are being crushed under its weight. *Baros* could refer to a physical or a spiritual problem. Burdens are obvious loads. Paul says, *"If you see someone who has a crushing and excessive boulder in their life, help them! Don't leave them!"*

I've had loads so heavy it felt like just breathing alone was more than I could bear. When I was deep in the pit of despair, being crushed by anxiety and depression, I could not help myself. I had to reach out for help—both to God, but also to my spiritual family. I needed them to carry my burden, making my pain bearable. Giving me courage so I could climb out of my pit of misery and to the Rock that was higher than I. I'm so thankful Paul wrote these words. It gives me such comfort.

Helping others do what they cannot do for themselves is sacrificial love. It honors God and fulfills the law of Christ. God commands it! If I'm going to be a follower of Christ, I must run to help those facing crushing loads. I am responsible "to" my brothers and sisters. We are each other's family, and when someone is hurting, we are all hurting. Our responsibility is to help them if we can.

"When someone is burdened by crushing cares and difficult events in life that are too much for one person to carry all by himself, crawl up under that burden and help that person carry it, and so fulfill the law of Christ."
- Rick Renner

God isn't asking us to help the person in need for a lifetime, rather, a directed time. *We'll talk more about this in a moment.*

WHAT ARE BACKPACKS?

Verse 5 states, ***"Each one should carry their own load."***

Why does Paul tell us in verse two to carry each other's burdens, and three verses later, he tells us to carry our own load? Is he confused?

We need to look at the Greek meaning to understand what Paul is saying. The word *"load"* means **a burden or cargo of daily toil.** It gives us a picture of a backpack. Paul is saying each of us should carry the backpack or the daily toil we've been given. He states we are all expected to carry our own load.

So, when we see someone working hard, laboring over their daily toil, we can be confident this is what God designed. Labor and hard work are part of God's plan. It's imperative we don't interrupt or step in the way.

**WE ARE RESPONSIBLE TO EACH OTHER
BUT NOT FOR EACH OTHER.**

If carrying each other's boulder is being responsible "to" someone, then letting someone carry their own burden and/or backpack is not being responsible "for" someone.

The Bible is saying we each are to carry our own load. But if someone gets in trouble with something too big to take care of on their own, we can step in for a moment and help them. But we are not created to carry everyone else's backpack. They are built to carry their own pack. We get in trouble when we take ownership of someone else's load.

God specifically designed a load for you. This backpack is part of His design, and it keeps us dependent upon Him for our daily happenings.

WHAT DO I NEED TO GIVE BACK?

So we have to ask ourselves these questions:

Am I carrying someone else's backpack around? Am I allowing myself to ease someone else's load, and it's keeping them a spiritual infant? Am I allowing them to grow in strength and endurance by carrying their own bag?

Secondly, *is there someone around me who has a crushing burden?* Am I expecting them to do something that I would not be able to do without help?

WE ARE RESPONSIBLE TO EACH OTHER BUT NOT FOR EACH OTHER.

Lastly, *is it time to give the burden back?* Was it a crushing boulder that has now become a backpack? Is it affecting the way I do life and my ability to carry my own load?

Today, I am hoping you will take some time and really evaluate and answer the questions above. God has not asked you to be a savior to the world. That role has already been taken by Himself.

As you have answered the questions above, I want you to understand something. If you've been holding someone else's backpack for a long time, you must assume you've not been able to carry your own load very well. God designed our lives only to carry our *backpack* and momentarily help others with their *burdens*. Not following God's order can leave us burned out, overwhelmed, and spiritually lazy.

Maybe you've been so used to carrying someone else's *daily toil* that you haven't been able to step in to help the *bigger burdens* of others that you're called to. *Did you catch that?*

When I carry someone else's backpack, my time, energy, and strength will be in jeopardy. When someone comes along with a burden, I won't have enough margin to help them. My resources will be extended.

When I give back the backpack, it frees me up to help others and live more obediently to God. When I carry someone else's daily load, I'm disobedient to God. I'm getting in the way of what God can do in and through me. God did not create me to carry more than I can bear. Relearning this will require more obedience. It will require an understanding that I am not more productive, more valuable, and more blessed because I'm doing things for others that they should be doing for themselves.

You may be getting in the way of what God is trying to do in them. I know this might be a new understanding to unpack, but it's now time to change. You know what is yours and what isn't.

To live a more powerful life, I will need to return the backpacks I've been carrying to their rightful owner. *What should I say?* Instead of feeling bad or that I'm being mean, what if I reframed in my heart and with my words. Something like, *"I'm learning to be more obedient to God by not holding this any longer for you."* or *"I'm crystal clear I am not responsible for this anymore. I'm giving it back to you, the rightful owner."*

REME MBER

+ Burdens are obvious loads.

+ Helping others do what they cannot do for themselves is sacrificial love. It honors God and fulfills the law of Christ.

+ We are responsible **to** each other, but not **for** each other.

+ God has not asked me to be a savior to the world. That role has already been taken by Himself.

+ I am called carry the backpack, or the daily toil, I've been given.

+ When I carry someone else's backpack, my time, energy, and strength will be in jeopardy, and I am not able to help others who have burdens, even if God directs me to do so.

+ When I carry someone else's backpack, I'm disobedient to God.

+ To live a more powerful life, I will need to return other people's backpacks.

"Carry each other's burdens, and in this way, you will fulfill the law of Christ." Galatians 6:2-5

Notice the focus isn't on **"expecting others to bear my burdens."** When I only look for others to carry my burdens, I'm *self-focused*. When my focus is solely on myself, it always leads to pride, frustration, discouragement, and depression.

Instead, God wants you and me to be *others-focused, and* this is why He says, "***Bear one another's burdens.***" A *simple* command to obey. Look for a brother or a sister with a burden, and help them with it. It isn't complicated. It doesn't take a vast program or massive infrastructure to pull it off.

I just look for a burden to bear and bear it. Period.

RESPOND

Remember the three questions I asked you earlier? Take some time to answer them here:

Am I carrying someone else's backpack (daily toil) around?

_____

_____

_____

Is there someone around me who has a crushing burden?

_____

_____

_____

If so, is it time to give the burden back?

_____

_____

_____

WEEK ONE
TAKEAWAYS

+ BEING NICE OUT OF FEAR DOESN'T WORK.

People pleasing will keep me stuck in the cycles of powerlessness that I am trying to break away from. My false power over other people's feelings and beliefs keeps me constantly trying to do the "right thing."

**+ BOUNDARIES KEEP THE GOOD
IN AND THE BAD OUT.**

Boundaries help us protect what matters most to us. They keep us from harm and protect safe and healthy love.

**+ GOD CREATED BOUNDARIES FOR THE SAKE
OF ORDER, OWNERSHIP, AND PROTECTION.**

Boundaries are in God's nature! He knows that when we have ownership, love is protected. When we allow love to motivate us, we can live whole lives by clearly knowing where we end and others begin. His Kingdom works!

**✛ GOD KNOWS IT'S POSSIBLE FOR ME
TO LIVE AN ABUNDANT LIFE WITHOUT
ANYONE ELSE PARTICIPATING.**

He holds me entirely responsible for my life. My beliefs,
emotions, and decisions all belong to me. I can see that as
a burden or I can see it as a position of power.

**✛ WE ARE RESPONSIBLE TO EACH OTHER,
BUT NOT FOR EACH OTHER.**

Labor and hard work are part of God's plan. It's imperative
we don't interrupt or step in the way. If carrying each
other's boulder is being responsible "to" someone, then
letting someone carry their own burden and/or backpack is
not being responsible "for" someone.

**FIND I DO BOUNDARIES STUDY VIDEOS ALONG
WITH OTHER RESOURCES AT TRUTHTOTABLE.COM**

AUTONOMY

"THINGS I OWN"

Welcome to Week Two!

I hope you had a chance to ask yourself the hard questions, examine the areas in your heart that need some attention, and find the courage to change.

Week Two is all about learning to keep the good in and the bad out. We'll discover what God holds me personally responsible for and how to act on my values.

Let's get started!

HOW DO I KEEP THE GOOD IN & THE BAD OUT?

"Above all else, guard your heart, for everything you do flows from it." Proverbs 4:23

Godly boundaries help us take care of our property. The Bible is clear when it tells us to be diligent with our lives. **"Guard your heart with all diligence."** (Proverbs 4:23)

BOUNDARIES HELP US KEEP THE GOOD IN AND THE BAD OUT.

They help us protect what is most important to us.

"Do not give dogs what is sacred; do not throw your pearls to pigs. If you do, they may trample them under their feet, and turn and tear you to pieces." Matthew 7:6 NIV

Simply stated, boundaries keep the good (pearls) in our lives and the bad (pigs) out.

Fast forward almost two years from that pivotal morning on the stage watching my newborn son disappear from my sight. I'm now a mom of two children that are 17 months apart. My marriage is four years young, and I'm still trying to navigate leading worship, speaking, mom'ing, and wife'ing.

Frankly, I was not doing well by the time our second son was three months old. I assumed it was because I had another C-section and my recovery was slow. Knowing that major surgeries can affect your mind and capacity, I gave it time. But I knew something wasn't right when time went on and my recovery was coming to an end.

BOUNDARIES HELP US KEEP THE GOOD IN AND THE BAD OUT.

One afternoon, at a pediatric appointment, I confessed to my pediatrician that I was not okay. I told her that taking a shower was the most I could do in a day. My sleeping was troubled and I lacked any and all motivation. It wasn't that I felt sad most days; it was that I felt nothing. I was humiliated by sharing such intimate details of my inner struggle. I figured, *why would she care?* Since she wasn't part of my church and I wasn't her pastor, I could dismiss her disapproval if she thought I was a bad mom or person.

But instead of shaming me or accusing me, she gently looked at me and said, *"I think you're dealing with postpartum depression."* I immediately knew she was right. I tried to hold back the tears that filled my eyes, knowing that any moment my face would contort into the "ugly cry."

I took a deep breath. Tears streaming down my face. I asked, *"What should I do?"* She explained that I needed to get help. I needed to talk to someone soon. She was right. I was determined to reach out for help. I was desperate.

Leaving the office, I took another deep breath, threw my shoulders back, and walked toward my car. After placing my son in his seat, all I could do was sit silently, letting the tears flow.

I couldn't believe I was here. *What was wrong with me?*

My thoughts trailed. *"Depression is not for Christian leaders, especially those focused on serving and pleasing God. Depression is for those who have made big mistakes causing severe regret. Depression is a consequence of bad living."*

I'm embarrassed to write these thoughts, but back then they were the true narrative in my mind. I knew I had postpartum depression and I didn't have the tools for healing. So, I sucked it up, picked up my phone, and called a friend's mom who I knew to be a Christian counselor in the area.

My message was simple, *"Heeelllooo ... hello Susan. My name is Havilah and I need some help. I just left my pediatrician's office and she recommended I give you a call. She's concerned I might be dealing with postpartum depression. Would I be able to come to talk to you? Just let me know. Thank you."*

I quickly hung up and headed home. As I pulled into my driveway, my phone rang. It was her. My anxiety rose as I clumsily answered. She was open to meeting with me. In fact, the next morning. My fear was still with me in the car, but now relief had joined us. I had no idea how this chain of events would alter my whole life.

I walked into her office the next morning and never left.

Ok, not quite.

I did go home that day, but I continued to go back. Our weekly meeting was my oxygen. I would gasp for air, filling my lungs just enough to make it to our next appointment. As the weeks went on, my capacity grew. I was getting better.

Six months later, I wasn't in survival mode anymore.

I thought I would be finished with counseling, but Susan asked if she could share something with me she felt I was ready to hear. Of course, I wanted to know. She said, *"Havilah, I believe you would've ended up in my office eventually. The baby just got you here sooner."* I sat there in disbelief. *What is she talking about? Doesn't she know that I'm a strong and capable person who has never had any issue before like this? Doesn't she understand that this was a situation that created my struggle?*

She went on. *"I think the best thing for you would be to commit another year with me. Learn more about healthy boundaries. Learn how to keep the good in and the bad out."*

She continued. *"I, myself, understand what it's like to be in ministry. My dad was a full-time minister and my husband as well. I understand the complexity of ministry life. I think I could really help you. Basically, I'm asking you to spend every Friday morning with me. I've gathered six other women who live in the city and need to learn the same tools. I have a few rules I would need you to abide by.*

First, I need a commitment from you to be here every Friday without fail. I'm going to teach you a lot of things that require you to learn them in sequence and it's important that you sacrifice to be here.

Second, every woman in the room must stay anonymous. Every one of you holds a highly influential role. It will allow you to relax, knowing everything you hear in this room must remain private and confidential."

I knew she was right. I then spent two full years learning, immersing myself in understanding, and implementing boundaries. I was a sponge. It changed my life forever. I want to help you, too, by sharing many of the things I learned. They SAVED MY LIFE.

FENCES . . . NOT WALLS

Firstly,

HEALTHY BOUNDARIES ARE FENCES, NOT WALLS.

They aren't barriers we've constructed to make our lives a fortress, a place where no one comes in and no one goes out. **Personal boundaries** are guidelines, rules, or limits that a person creates to identify reasonable, safe, and permissible ways for other people to behave toward them. They teach us how to respond when someone passes those limits. Boundaries are created to help us stay safe in the relationship rather than keeping us safe outside of the community.

BOUNDARIES KEEP OUR CONNECTIONS STRONG. THEY HELP US PROTECT LOVE BY TAKING OWNERSHIP AND RESPONSIBILITY.

I'd always assumed people who could aggressively communicate their rules had strong boundaries. It's not true. Your level of strength and aggression does not mean you have safe boundaries. Just because I can say "NO" doesn't mean I have nothing else to learn. There's a lot more to creating healthy boundaries than being born with the right personality.

I've seen people use the word "boundaries" as a way to keep people away from them. They end up living an isolated life. We don't love people well when we live like this. We keep them far away so we don't have to experience negative feelings. We've constructed cement walls rather than breathable boundaries. Healthy boundaries are not cement walls to keep everyone and everything out; they move, live and breathe with you.

"In Him we live and move and have our being." Acts 17:28

Healthy boundaries are not cement walls to keep everyone and everything out. Second, Godly boundaries have gates that swing both ways. Personal boundaries operate in two directions, affecting both the incoming and outgoing interactions between people. These are sometimes referred to as "protection" and "containment" functions in order to keep the bad out while inviting the good to stay close.

REME MBER

+ Godly boundaries help me take care of my property (what God has given me).

+ Boundaries help me protect what is most important.

+ **Healthy boundaries are fences, not walls.**

+ Boundaries keep my connections strong by helping me protect love by taking ownership and responsibility.

+ There's a lot more to creating healthy boundaries than being born with the right personality.

Dr. Nina Brown, a counselor, professor, and prolific author, describes four types of boundaries people have: soft, rigid, spongy, or flexible.

Soft – A person with soft boundaries merges with other people's boundaries. Someone with a soft boundary is easily a victim of psychological manipulation.

Spongy – A person with spongy boundaries has a combination of soft and rigid boundaries. Spongy boundaries permit less emotional contagion than soft boundaries, but are more flexible than rigid boundaries. People with spongy boundaries are often unsure of what to let in and what to keep out.

Rigid – A person with rigid boundaries is closed or walled off so no one can get close to them, either physically or emotionally. This is often the case if someone has been the victim of physical, emotional, psychological, or sexual abuse. Rigid boundaries can be **selective,** and are dependent on time, place or circumstances. This is usually because of a previous bad experience in a similar situation.

Flexible – a person with flexible boundaries has both spongy and rigid boundaries, but exercises more control. They continually discern what to let in and what to keep out. Consequently, they are more resistant to emotional contagion and psychological manipulation, and are difficult to exploit.

RESPOND

Identify which boundaries you have from above!

Soft, Spongy, Rigid, or Flexible.

DAY SEVEN

WHAT SHOULD I BE FOCUSING ON?

Last week, we discovered that boundaries are essential to living a healthy life.

As a spiritual grown-up, my boundaries keep me protected. They make my life manageable; and when my life is manageable, I'm shielded from living burned out, overworked, and having others take advantage of me. Life becomes enjoyable again, because I'm living the way God designed.

Regardless of whether our pride, insecurity, or wrong theology brought us to this place, it's not too late to understand the power of healthy boundaries. It's never too late to experience the joy of knowing you're living exactly as God intended. There is a deep comfort in knowing God doesn't give us more than we can bear.

Yesterday, we looked at why our walls need to be breathable and flexible.

We're not constructing walls built to keep everything out. We're creating living and breathing boundaries that help us steward the places God holds us responsible for. Our areas of ownership.

We spent time understanding personal boundaries and where property lines exist. Today, we're going to take a different perspective.

God has designed a specific property for you alone. Let's call it your "yard."

My yard has an invisible gate around it and within it lies the things God holds me personally responsible for. When I get to heaven, God will ask me how I stewarded these specific areas. He knows **I'm 100% the owner of these things, which means I have 100% authority and anointing to lead these areas.**

THERE IS A DEEP COMFORT IN KNOWING GOD DOESN'T GIVE US MORE THAN WE CAN BEAR.

Even if we've never been taught these things before, we will begin to see what God sees. We can manage what He is asking of us well if we give it our full attention. In fact, we will have very little time for anything else if we take on full ownership.

WHAT'S INSIDE MY YARD?

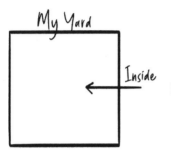

"Now may the God of peace make you holy in every way, and may your whole spirit and soul and body be kept blameless until our Lord Jesus Christ comes again."
1 Thessalonians 5:23 (NLT)

In 1 Thessalonians 5:23, it says I am a triune being. My life contains three parts: a spirit, a soul, and a body. If God is making me "holy in every way," then all three parts have the ability to contain God and be filled by Him.

Having been filled by Him, out of the overflow, I can't help but express who He is to those around me. I am a spiritual being. As a hand fits inside a glove, so God's Spirit fits inside my spirit. My spirit was made to fully contain God! Not all He is, but all I need Him to be at any given moment.

Today we're going to focus on one of the three areas - *our spirit.*

MY SPIRIT

TRANSFORMS FROM DEATH TO LIFE

The Bible says that each of us has a spirit and that spirit was lifeless until Christ came to fill it. Picture your spirit as a deflated balloon that was dead to God. Then when you were "made alive" in Christ (1 Peter 3:18), the balloon was filled with God's Spirit. Your spirit inflated with Him and became BIG inside of you. Jesus made a way for us to live a filled and fulfilled life. He was the bridge between us having a dead spirit or an alive spirit.

Kevin was a guy who wandered into our church years ago. He'd been living a new age/guru lifestyle. His clothes mimicked festival attire, his hair was relaxed with sun-bleached tips. He wore flip-flops with a guitar slung over his shoulder.

He walked in wide-eyed, eager to learn. The atmosphere immediately grabbed his attention. His curiosity led him to live a pretty extraordinary life by the age of 28. He and his other traveling friends had searched for spiritual awakenings in everything from music, holistic living, and occasional marijuana use.

He was likable. Immediately his big smile filled his face, and it was easy to imagine his 12-year-old self. He was curious about the music and the warm faces. The communal engagement. Kevin hadn't ever been to a church, so he didn't have any context.

Our conversations quickly evolved to faith, Christianity, and spirituality.

We explained that we, as Christ followers, didn't believe there are multiple ways to Heaven. The Bible was clear that there was one way to the Father, and that was through believing in Jesus Christ, the Son of God. We accepted that there was no way to fix our sinful nature on our own and we needed a Savior. Jesus was the Way! We were living under the Lordship of Jesus Christ.

Now, we had Kevin's curiosity even more. Ready to try anything, Kevin jumped in to attend our gatherings.

Weeks turned into months, and with every moment, Kevin was chewing on more significant pieces. Eventually, one night at the end of worship, our pastor gave an invitation to anyone in the room who wanted a relationship with God. Anyone who had found themselves at a desperate place, having tried everything but still not filling the deep hole inside.

Kevin slipped his hand up that night. Tears streamed down his face and you could see the tangible presence of God resting upon him. Kevin had been awakened for the first time. It wasn't some momentary euphoria or an experience to add to a list of other exotic experiences. No! Kevin had a radical encounter with the love of Jesus that night. He lifted his hands and there was a divine exchange. Sadness for joy. Brokenness for healing. Fatherlessness for a Heavenly Father that knew him and loved him. Kevin was never the same again.

Today, Kevin leads his own church. His church is full of other young seekers, just as he was those 16 years ago. But Kevin's resolve has never changed. His spirit was dead but now it's alive.

As you read the story about Kevin, I want you to see how boundaries operate in our lives. These boundaries allow the Holy Spirit to do His job without us getting in the way.

Let's answer a question together, **"What do boundaries look like for our spiritual life?"**

Let's start here:

Whose job is it to draw the unbeliever to God?

Whose job is to save people?

Whose job is to ask the Father to help us?

Life gets so much easier when we become crystal clear on these answers. We can go back to enjoying our abundant life. Let's continue looking at what the Holy Spirit does and we'll answer these questions afterwards.

COMMUNICATES WITH GOD

Your spirit communicates with God the Father because Spirit talks to spirit. Your 'alive' spirit gives you the ability to hear the Holy Spirit's voice and understand His thoughts.

> **"You will receive power when the Holy Spirit comes on you, and you will be my witness... to the ends of the earth."**
> **Acts 1:8 (NIV)**

The Holy Spirit is God's presence within us. He is part of the Trinity (the Father, the Son, and the Holy Spirit). The Holy Spirit is supernatural and all-powerful. He knows everything, and isn't limited by time and space.

EMPOWERS SPIRIT-LED LIVING

Yes, there is a God-shaped hole in each of us until the Holy Spirit comes and fills it. But there's more! The Spirit of God invites you and me to "live and move and have our being" in Him **(Acts 17:28, NIV)**. It's not dependent on what we can contain. We're invited to come into the full Kingdom of God and the culture of Heaven.

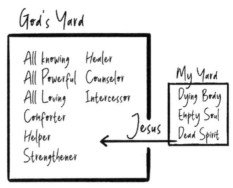

We step into the YARD of GOD. We live "in" Christ. (Romans 6:8) Covered in the righteousness of Christ, a new creation, and a chosen people. (2 Corinthians 5:17, 1 Peter 2:9, Romans 3:22)

Our brokenness is brought into the Yard of an all-knowing, all-powerful, loving, comforting, healing, and hope-filled God. Our small, ruined, bankrupt yard is now in God's world. Our life radically changes because we now have access to God's "anything is possible" yard!

So when it comes to vibrant living, the Holy Spirit in you brings that vibrancy and abundance from Heaven to your heart and life.

"But when he, the Spirit of truth, comes, he will guide you into all the truth. He will not speak on his own; he will speak only what he hears, and he will tell you what is yet to come. He will glorify me because it is from me that he will receive what he will make known to you."
John 16:13-14 (NIV)

OFFERS AUTHENTIC POWER

You now have authentic power available to you at any given moment of the day because the Holy Spirit fills you.

REME MBER

+ I'm 100% the owner of my yard, which means I have 100% authority and anointing over my property.

+ I am a triune being. My life contains three parts: a spirit, a soul, and a body.

+ I am "made alive" in Christ.

+ My spirit communicates with God because Spirit talks to spirit.

+ The Holy Spirit in me brings that vibrancy and abundance from Heaven to my heart and life.

+ Jesus says that the Holy Spirit was sent to "act on His behalf" and in His place.

READ

When we depend on personal strength to live our Christian life, we're shutting out the Holy Spirit, and Paul calls this very unwise.

> **"Are you so foolish? After beginning with the Spirit, are you now trying to attain your goal by human effort?"**
> **Galatians 3:3 (NIV)**

The results of ignoring the Spirit and His help, and living life on our own, are painful; filled with worry, bad attitudes, destructive habits, lust, rebellion, jealousy, unhealthy relationships, etc. We each have our own list.

The most powerful thing I can do is get clear on what God can and will do and know what I can't do. Let's answer the questions above with a simple, ***"What do boundaries look like for our Spiritual life?"***

RESPOND

Let's do an exercise to help us walk this out!

I want you to take some time to fill out your *Ownership Sheet.*

Look through Kevin's story and write down what was in your yard and what was God's yard.

My Spirit
(ownership sheet)

I Own

- Dead/Deflated
- Communicates w/ Holy Spirit
- Ask for Power
- I Do What He Says

God Owns

- Alive/Filled
- Holy Spirit Communicates w/ God the Father
- Gives Power + Authority
- Tells me What to do

AM I DEAD ON THE INSIDE?

"Ouch!" It was starting to hurt as I spoke, feeling the tenderness on the sides of my throat. My voice was beginning to sound raspy. If this continued, I was confident my voice would be gone by the end of the day.

"I can't believe this is happening again (deep sigh). I really need my voice." I could feel the anxiety rolling up my body and my chest was starting to feel tight.

Scheduled to lead worship at all weekend services, which included up to seven hours on a microphone, I was in trouble. *"Oh, and I have that baby shower after church."* My thoughts continued. *"I'm in serious trouble."* Then it hits me, *"OH MY GOSH, I leave for vacation on Monday."* Now my body and mind were in a full-blown panic. *"I'll be lucky to have a voice by Sunday evening, and I'll be struggling to talk for God knows how long on my trip."*

This scenario happened for almost two years now. Losing my voice frequently was now hurting my ability to function; after all, talking was part of the job.

Finally, I went to see a nose, throat, and ear doctor. She scoped my nose and throat. Yes, it's exactly as it sounds. The doctor gently inserts the scope through one nostril then closely inspects your nose, throat, and larynx.

I found out I had nodules on both vocal cords that day. The sores on my vocal cords evolved from blisters to calluses. I'd been back every other week for almost a year, hoping for some improvement.

Nothing.

The doctor was finally suggesting a last-ditch effort of surgery. She would go inside to remove both calluses.

Normally, I wouldn't know anything about this, but actress Julie Andrews had just been through a surgery, according to the media. News spread that the doctors botched her throat surgery. Fearing I might never have my voice again, I decided I wouldn't do it. I never returned.

Weeks later, the music teacher from the Christian school approached me. *"I've heard about some of the problems you're having with your voice. I think I can help."*

I was just about ready to try anything.

He continued, *"I've watched you speak, answer phones, and talk in the office. You really punch your words. You force them out. You also make a lot of character voices in your storytelling, which is extremely hard on your voice."* Frankly, I'd always assumed it was my singing that damaged my voice, never my speaking.

"When your voice sounds tired, I suggest you rest at all costs. Monitor the punchiness of your words. The moment you start to feel fatigued, STOP talking.

Go to bed.

Leave the party.

Get a good night's sleep.

Also, keep your throat nice and warm. If it's cold outside, wear a scarf around your neck. Drink warm water. But most of all, don't whisper. If you have any sign you're losing your voice, stop what you are doing immediately."

Having nothing to lose, I did what he recommended. It was hard work. As a 20-something, I was accustomed to staying up late, burning the candle at both ends. I was in trouble, and I needed to make significant changes.

PHYSICAL IS SPIRITUAL

Twenty years later, I still put to practice what I learned. Every day. There was no quick fix. No surgery. The daily discipline to guard and monitor my own body was the secret to my success in having a voice. I rarely lose my voice now. It's a thing of the past because **my daily discipline protects me.**

WHAT'S INSIDE MY YARD?

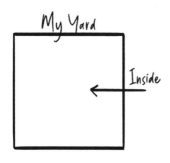

"Now may the God of peace make you holy in every way, and may your whole spirit and soul and body be kept blameless until our Lord Jesus Christ comes again."
1 Thessalonians 5:23 (NLT)

Yesterday, we looked at 1 Thessalonians 5:23 together and we saw that God gives us three critical areas to take ownership. They are my stewardship. My responsibility. My yard contains three parts; a spirit, a soul, and a body.

We've looked at our spirit, but today we're going to look at our bodies. He has given you ownership of everything including your physical frame.

Learning to steward your body is very spiritual.

Look at the words of Paul,

"The physical part of you is not some piece of property belonging to the spiritual part of you. God owns the

LEARNING TO STEWARD YOUR BODY IS VERY SPIRITUAL.

whole works. So let people see God in and through your body."
1 Corinthians 6:19 (MSG)

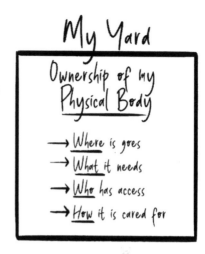

My Yard

Ownership of my Physical Body

→ Where is goes
→ What it needs
→ Who has access
→ How it is cared for

We've learned that the Holy Spirit inhabits our spirit. Well, God also says that the body He gave you is a place where He dwells. It's a temple!

The NIV translates the above scripture like this:

"Do you not know that your bodies are temples of the Holy Spirit, who is in you, whom you have received from God? You are not your own; you were bought at a price. Therefore honor God with your bodies."
1 Corinthians 6:19 (NIV)

It's important to understand that your body, soul, and spirit all contain the Spirit of God. He gets to inhabit the whole of me! It's vitally important to realize how intrinsically connected each part is to the others. Therefore, it is impossible to do something with your body that doesn't affect your soul and spirit.

We can often believe we are having a spiritual issue when it really originated in the physical. My postpartum depression wasn't primarily a spiritual deficiency, it was predominantly physical. But, it took me taking responsibility for my whole being and treating my physical struggle, in order to see how it was connected to my spirit.

Jesus lived the same way!

JESUS ACCEPTED HIS PHYSICAL LIMITS

JESUS MET HIS PERSONAL NEEDS.

He ate healthy food, got the sleep He needed, and even took naps. He took the time to relax and did a lot of walking. *(Matt 26:18, 20; Mark 1:16, 3:23, 4:38; Luke 7:36; John 10:40, 12:2)*

JESUS ENJOYED TIME ALONE.

He withdrew from the crowds to go away on retreat, alone or with friends. (Luke 4:1-2, 14-15, Mark 6:30-32, Matthew 14:1-13, Luke 6:12-13, Luke 5:16)

JESUS RECEIVED SUPPORT FROM FRIENDS.

He initiated companionship with friends. (Matt 26:36-38)

JESUS LIVED AN UNHURRIED PACE OF LIFE.

He was never in a hurry. Not even to go to Jerusalem and embrace His cross. The will of His Father was all He wanted to do. *(John 11:6; Mark 10:32)*

JESUS SURRENDERED THE OUTCOME TO GOD.

"Jesus was tempted to become paralyzed with fear about the cross. Satan and his demons, along with many people who hated him, were trying to kill him. Would he make it to the cross to die for us, to be 'lifted up' publicly so it draws people to God? He let go. He chose not to force things, but to trust

*the Father's will. To the Father, he abandoned the outcomes
of his sufferings and trials to come, as he always did."*
(Mark 14:32-42)

HEALTHY PHYSICAL BOUNDARIES

We can learn a lot from the life of Jesus.

Here's a few more physical boundaries. *Consider adding
your own boundaries in a journal!*

MY BODY HAS LIMITS.

Experiencing physical limits can be very frustrating. We can
live exhausted, burned out, and drained. This can leave us
feeling so discouraged or even embarrassed that we ignore
our limitations altogether, or run ourselves ragged until we
can't do another thing.

Stewardship is respecting the full function along with
embracing the limitations. It's ridiculous to be frustrated
that I can't reach something because of my height. It's
equally absurd to hold ourselves to an unattainable
standard that God hasn't asked or made possible. Relax.
Everyone has limits. Promise.

MY BODY NEEDS SAFETY.

I can't abuse my body and expect God to take care of it.
Taking care of my body and keeping it safe is under my list
of responsibilities. Take a deep breath. If God gives it to me,
He's given me everything I need to make it happen. But
only in His timing.

Taking care of my body is something He wants to help me
do.

With that said, there are things entirely out of my control. Some of us were born with limitations. Some of us were victims of abuse from another. This was never your fault and this was never God's plan; however, it can change the way we think of our bodies. God can and will use every bad thing in our life and turn it into good if we allow Him. Healing is ours for the taking, and with the help of God and counseling we no longer need to live in the same fear or pain we once did. Others of us have abused our bodies and changed them forever. But abuse doesn't need to get the last word in our story.

You can start today. I love the quote, **"When we know better, we do better."** You can see your physical body as connected to your spiritual life and allow God to show you what it looks like to care for His most incredible creation... YOU.

REME MBER

+ Daily disciplines to guard and monitor my body are the secret to success.

+ Daily disciplines are essential.

+ Part of my stewardship and ownership is my physical body.

+ Learning to steward my body is very spiritual.

+ The body God gave me is a place where He dwells. It's a temple!

+ It's impossible to do something with my body that doesn't touch and affect my soul and spirit.

+ God views my body as a place of holiness.

+ I will not allow my body to disqualify me.

OWNERSHIP REQUIRES DAILY DISCIPLINE

When it comes to living a healthy life, which **Ephesians 1:4** tells us we are called to do, we must understand this includes our whole being. Your body is valuable to God because it houses Him and, therefore, the way you care for and protect it matters to God. He views your body as a place of holiness. I love the verse in the Bible that talks about being an athlete.

> **"So I run with purpose in every step. I am not just shadow boxing. I discipline my body like an athlete, training it to do what it should. Otherwise, I fear that after preaching to others I myself might be disqualified."**
> **1 Corinthians 9:26–27 (NLT)**

What Paul is describing is one of his core values. That he leads his body, not the other way around. We have to renew our heart, our mind, and our will. We have to discipline our bodies. Paul disciplines his body because he knows it has the potential to lead him astray. He is in charge of his body, and in this scripture, it's clear that this is not up for debate! He will not allow his body to disqualify him.

I have small children around the house. At least a few times a week, you will hear me say, *"I am the boss of you!"* I say it jokingly, of course, but it gets the message across. I'm essentially saying, *"I'm in charge, in case you're wondering!"*

I DO BOUNDARIES

Paul is basically saying this to himself, and then he is explaining his internal narrative to benefit you and me. It sounds like, *"Body, I tell you what you can and cannot do. You are not in charge. I am the boss of you."*

As the owner and steward of my body, identifying some practical boundaries can help protect what matters most.

RESPOND

Today, I want us to confess to our physical bodies.

We've said enough negative things. Let's start declaring positive things.

"I would love to do everything and be everywhere. But God, the Creator of my physical body, did not make that possible. I want to be here for the long haul! I want to live a long and prosperous life, which means I can't sacrifice my physical needs on the altar of human expectation. It's my responsibility to take care of my body.

So, I'm going to be honest about what I can and can't do. I'm choosing to trust God with the rest. I'm treating my body with the love and respect it deserves. I'm going to focus on feeding it wholesome food, healthy hydration, and the nourishment my body needs to live a long life.

I'm going to make sure I'm getting a good night's sleep. Creating and keeping the Sabbath and giving time for rest and celebration.

Thank you, God, for meeting all of my physical needs. Thank you for healing me. Restoring me. And giving me a long life.

I confess this by faith, in Jesus' name!"

DAY NINE

WHY IS EVERYTHING I'M DOING NOT WORKING?

"You don't have a soul. You are a soul. You have a body."
C.S. Lewis

WHAT'S INSIDE MY YARD?

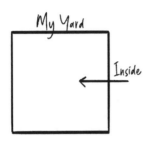

My Yard

Inside

"Now may the God of peace make you holy in every way, and may your whole spirit and soul and body be kept blameless until our Lord Jesus Christ comes again."
1 Thessalonians 5:23 (NLT)

In 1 Thessalonians 5:23, it says I am a triune being. My life contains three parts; a spirit, a soul, and a body. **Today, we are going to look at the final place of ownership God gives us.**

My Yard
Dying Body
Empty Soul
Dead Spirit

Let's do a quick review.

First, **God gave me a spirit.**

My spirit was dead until I invited Jesus to come in and fill me. My spirit has very specific and incredible ways it engages with God.

1. After I invite God to come in and live inside me, He brings to life everything lifeless.

2. I have the privilege of communicating with God through the Holy Spirit. The Holy Spirit speaks to my Heavenly Father on my behalf.

3. I have access to everything in God's YARD. I can activate His Kingdom in my life, anytime and anywhere.

Second, **God gave me a physical body.**

My body may be dying on the Earth but is transformed in eternity. Even though it's not a perfect body, the Holy Spirit lives within. He has given me complete ownership of my body. Part of stewarding well is answering these questions:

1. What does my body need?

2. Where does my body go?

3. Who has access to my body?

4. How can I care for my body?

Lastly, we're going to look at our final section of ownership: **my soul.**

In Genesis 2:7 it says that Man was created as a "living soul." Your soul makes up your mind, your will, and your emotions. This is very different from your spirit. Your soul is the place where regeneration takes place.

Here's what I mean...

When Christ comes to live inside of you, your spirit becomes "born-again." At once! It doesn't need to be regenerated because it is brand new and works perfectly.

The Bible says you are a new creation.

Romans 6:7–11 says that you are no longer bound by sin or enslaved to it, but have an ability to live a life free from sin and all the destruction and devastation that comes with it.

"For when we died with Christ we were set free from the power of sin... We are sure of this because Christ was raised from the dead, and he will never die again... When he died, he died once to break the power of sin... So you also should consider yourselves to be dead to the power of sin."
Romans 6:7–11 (NLT)

Your mind, your will, and your emotions (your soul), on the other hand, must be transformed. *How do we know this?*

Romans 12:2 encourages us to be transformed by a renewing process:

"...let God transform you into a new person by changing the way you think." Romans 12:2 (NLT)

Or even better, The Message says,

"...fix your attention on God. You'll be changed from the inside out. Readily recognize what he wants from you, and quickly respond to it." Romans 12:2 (MSG)

Romans is saying that when we renew our minds, we will know the will of God for our lives. Perhaps our greatest struggle isn't God speaking to us, but rather renewing our minds enough to actually hear Him. Transformation awakens us to the transactions of Heaven. It opens our eyes and ears to listen to what God is saying and doing.

In 2 Corinthians 10:5-6, it clarifies that the kind of renewal we are called to is from the inside out. It says that it involves casting down arguments and getting rid of wrong thoughts that keep us from God; setting our thoughts on Him and keeping them there.

> **"We use our powerful God-tools for ... fitting every loose thought and emotion and impulse into the structure of life shaped by Christ. Our tools are ready at hand for clearing the ground of every obstruction and building lives of obedience into maturity." 2 Corinthians 10:5-6 (MSG)**

I like to say, *"Your mind has a mind of its own."*

Most Christians get discouraged right here. We think that what we've received isn't working. We believe our struggle is with the behavior of sinning, but really it's with the process of renewal.

Last week, we took our kids to a Go-Kart track. Our boys were finally all big enough to drive their own cars. As all six of us ran to get in line, the boys quickly declared what car they would drive and what color they would pick.

Mom and Dad were left with the last two.

When the flag went down, we all shot forward in our cars. But I quickly noticed one of our sons was having a hard time getting his car to move forward. As we rounded the track multiple times, we called to him, *"Put your foot on the gas! Push down as hard as you can so you can go faster!"*

When the timer finally ran out, we all parked our cars and got out. To which our son burst into tears. Tears streamed down his face as he quickly announced, *"My car is broken! It wouldn't go. I didn't get the same car you all got."*

We wanted to sympathize with him but knew he was wrong. We all had the same exact car. The issue was his capacity. We knew that if we could have gotten him to push the pedal harder, his car would have driven as fast as everybody else's.

We often act like this in our spiritual lives.

On the track of life, we are all trying to round the corners and head for the finish line. But many of us can't get our cars to move forward. We declare we didn't get what everybody else got. The Christian life didn't work for us.

I wish I could agree with you to make you feel better, but

THE TRUTH IS WE HAVE ALL BEEN GIVEN EVERYTHING WE NEED TO LIVE AN ABUNDANT LIFE.

"By his divine power, God has given us everything we need for living a godly life. We have received all of this by coming to know him, the one who called us to himself by means of his marvelous glory and excellence." 2 Peter 1:3 (NLT)

Living the abundant life has everything to do with how we function.

It has to do with what we're willing to do in order to learn to move and live and have our being.

WE HAVE ALL BEEN GIVEN EVERYTHING WE NEED TO LIVE AN ABUNDANT LIFE.

If we get distracted in our spiritual lives by believing our cars are broken, we won't ever learn the strategies and tools for living the transformed life.

Transformation is where we partner with God.

We aren't the author or the finisher, but we are the drivers.

We're the athletes and we have to run.

So if you're struggling, I suggest it's not a broken car but rather a problem with strategy. *You've stalled out at transformation.*

The writer of Proverbs puts it like this:

"Above all else, guard your heart, for everything you do flows from it." Proverbs 4:23 (NIV)

We see here that the heart [1] is central to our lives and is the seat of our emotions and will. Simply put, our emotions and our will must be renewed as well as our minds.

"A natural (soulish) man does not accept the things of the Spirit of God, for they are foolishness to him; and he cannot understand them, because they are spiritually appraised (discerned only through the Spirit.)"
1 Corinthians 2:14 (NASB)

If our soul is not renewed and brought under our spirit man's governing, then we won't be able to discern what God is doing in our lives.

"Toxic thoughts in your mind will poison your spirit and your soul." —Beni Johnson

---

1 The heart, according to the Bible, is part of man's spiritual makeup. It is the place where emotions and desires begin; it is that which drives the will of man towards action.

So what does transformation look like when it comes to our soul?

Simply put:

MY MIND IS RENEWED:

Taking every thought captive. (2 Corinthians 10:5)

Casting down wrong thinking. (2 Corinthians 10:5)

Receiving the mind of Christ. (1 Corinthians 2:16)

Knowing the will of God. (Romans 12:2)

MY EMOTIONS ARE HEALED:

PEACE: Anxiety will go and I will have peace beyond my understanding. (Philippians 4:6-7)

REST: I can lay my cares and worries before God. He will give me rest for my weary soul. (Matthew 11:28)

COMFORT: He will wipe every tear from my eyes and comfort me. (Revelation 21:4)

HELP: God is my refuge and strength, an ever-present help in trouble. (Psalm 46:1-2)

MY WILL SURRENDERED

Jesus prayed in the Garden of Gethsemane, saying, *"Father, if it is Your will, take this cup away from Me; nevertheless, not My will, but Yours, be done."* Jesus didn't get a new will. He didn't change His desire. He told His Father His preference, but surrendered His will to His Father's ultimate plan. If we want to live a transformed life, surrender is the way forward. (Matthew 26:39)

We may not fully understand it, but we know God's will is always meant to prosper us. (Jeremiah 29:11)

REME
MBER

+ Man was created as a "living soul." My soul is made up of my mind, my will, and my emotions.

+ My soul is the place where regeneration takes place.

+ When Christ comes to live inside of me, my spirit becomes "born-again." At once! It doesn't need to be regenerated because it is brand new and works perfectly.

+ My mind, my will, and my emotions (my soul) must be transformed.

+ We believe our struggle is with the behavior of sinning, but really it's with the process of renewal.

+ If my soul is not renewed and brought under our spirit man's governing, then I won't be able to discern what God is doing in our lives.

+ Transformation of my soul looks like a renewed mind, healed emotions, and a surrendered will.

"Carry one another's burdens and in this way you will fulfill the requirements of the law of Christ [that is, the law of Christian love]. 3 For if anyone thinks he is something [special] when [in fact] he is nothing [special except in his own eyes], he deceives himself. 4 But each one must carefully scrutinize his own work [examining his actions, attitudes, and behavior], and then he can have the personal satisfaction and inner joy of doing something commendable without comparing himself to another. 5 For every person will have to bear [with patience] his own burden [of faults and shortcomings for which he alone is responsible].
Galatians 6:2-5 Amplified Bible

Let's revisit verse 4.

We talked about this on Day Five, but I want you to notice how the author encourages us to carefully examine our own work.

IT GIVES US THREE SPECIFIC THINGS TO SCRUTINIZE:

1. We are to assess our actions.

2. We are to check our attitudes.

3. We are to examine our behaviors.

During the next three days, we are going to spend time talking about these three areas. I'm so excited to jump into this section!

RESPOND

TAKE WHAT YOU NEED!

Have you ever seen ads on a bulletin board where they have their cell number listed multiple times at the bottom for people to tear off and take with them? Think of this as your mental take away for emotions. From the list below, identify what you need and pray accordingly!

PEACE: Anxiety will go and I will have peace beyond my understanding.

Don't be pulled in different directions or worried about a thing. Be saturated in prayer throughout each day, offering your faith-filled requests before God with overflowing gratitude. Tell him every detail of your life, then God's wonderful peace that transcends human understanding, will make the answers known to you through Jesus Christ. Philippians 4:6-7 (TPT)

REST: I can lay my cares and worries before God. He will give me rest for my weary soul.

Come to me, all you who are weary and burdened, and I will give you rest. Matthew 11:28 (NIV)

COMFORT: He will wipe every tear from my eyes and He will comfort me.

He will wipe every tear from their eyes. There will be no more death or mourning or crying or pain, for the old order of things has passed away. Revelation 21:4 (NIV)

HELP: God is my refuge and strength, an ever-present help in trouble.

God, you're such a safe and powerful place to find refuge! You're a proven help in time of trouble— more than enough and always available whenever I need you. So we will never fear even if every structure of support were to crumble away. We will not fear even when the earth quakes and shakes, moving mountains and casting them into the sea. Psalm 46:1-2 (TPT)

WHY AM I FEELING THIS WAY?

I was doing it again. I was sabotaging my relationships.

I couldn't help it. It felt so real, so personal.

Didn't they know they were hurting my feelings?

Didn't they know how incredibly insensitive they were acting?

It all started a month before when we decided to go to dinner as girlfriends. A girl's night out! Who wouldn't say "yes" to a childless, spouse-free, and all the real food you can eat kind-of-meal?

Quickly picking the date and time, I couldn't contain my excitement!

As the evening came around, I was full of anticipation. I jumped in my car and headed to the restaurant. Arriving a few minutes early, I grabbed my phone to check my messages.

"Wait... WHAT? What are all these text messages?" A full text thread in the last hour informing me that everyone had canceled. Plans changed. No one would be coming.

I was the last to know.

Of course, I could have checked my phone, but it's not often a priority when you're trying to get out of a house full of kids.

I could feel my eyes fill with tears.

"Havilah, you cannot cry. Are you serious?" I thought, scolding myself.

I was embarrassed. Humiliated I was having this reaction.

"You're a full-grown adult, and now you're crying because your friends can't make it tonight? Junior high called; they asked how you're doing." Sarcasm.

I wiped the tears away, hoping not to smudge my makeup.

Sitting in the silence, I could feel anger now.

"How could they even have time to be on their phones? Didn't they have to take care of their families like me? Clearly, I'm a better mom."

I was attacking now. There it was; the ugly side of me.

Taking a deep breath, I realized, *"You are making the biggest deal out of the smallest thing, Havilah. Get it together! Haven't we been here before?"*

Immediately, I could think of multiple times I felt this way in the past year.

It wasn't the exact scenario, but it was the identical feelings.

I knew I needed to start by asking myself a few questions. I was looking for self-awareness. Working hard over the past years, I'd grown in this area. I knew better than to shove it down, hoping it went away.

First question, *"Why is this affecting you so much?"*

Second question, *"Have these friends done this to you before? Is this really their reputation?"*

I knew they hadn't. My friends had been good to me. Not perfect, but definitely not vicious.

Back to the first question, *"Okay, yes, this feeling feels familiar."* My mind wandered back to memories of junior high. The feelings of being left out. Uninvited. Overlooked. They were all familiar.

"Okay, Havilah, let's focus on the truth." ... "What is true about you?"

I was good at this part. I'd worked hard to get this deep inside me.

"I am loved. I am worthy. I'm a child of God. I believe the best. Everyone is doing the best they can. No one set out to hurt me. I'm sad. Disappointed. Those feelings are totally normal."

I could feel my emotions subsiding, and I was beginning to feel hope again. I laughed. I wasn't mocking; I was giving myself permission to be who I was, where I was. I laughed at myself because I know I'm dramatic and intense.

Within a few minutes, I began to feel peace. An inner peace that says, *"It's okay for things not to happen the way you wanted them to. Plus, your friends really do love you and are doing their best."*

OWN YOUR FEELINGS

I spent many years feeling bad about feeling bad.

I dismissed my emotions, believing my feelings were flawed. When I finally understood, "MY feelings were in MY yard," I was set free! I discovered the power and authority to guide them into truth.

Some of my story needed healing. When I experienced healing, my feelings changed. They didn't cancel my beliefs or override my confidence, but triggered me to even more healing and transformation.

WHAT DOES GOD THINK ABOUT FEELINGS?

GOD ISN'T NEUTRAL ABOUT OUR FEELINGS. HE ENDORSES THEM.

Have you ever stopped to think why God would put this verse in the Bible?

"Jesus wept." (John 11:35)

The shortest verse in the entire Bible might hold the most significant meaning. Jesus, who was fully God and fully man, had emotions just like us. He allowed Himself to cry. This verse shows us that He gave Himself permission to acknowledge and accept his feelings. Hopefully, it permits us to experience our emotions without shame.

Here are a few Biblical stats of emotions used in the Bible:

+ The word "anger" is mentioned 270 times in the Bible.

+ The word "joy" is mentioned 242 times.

+ "Grief" is mentioned 35 times.

GOD ISN'T NEUTRAL ABOUT OUR FEELINGS.

HE ENDORSES THEM.

+ "Mourning" is mentioned 47 times, and "mourn" is mentioned 138 times.

+ "Sadness" is only mentioned once, and "frightened" is only mentioned 9 times.

+ "Terror" is mentioned 88 times.

STEWARDING YOUR SOUL

Your soul has three specific areas of stewardship.

The first area of ownership is your **feelings**. Your feelings are in your yard. They are entirely yours and chosen by you. You have the right to feel whatever you want to feel. I love the quote that says, *"Feelings are like waves. You get to decide which one you want to ride to the beach."*

NO MORAL VALUE

The excellent news is emotions have no moral value.

Why else would the Bible say...

"Be angry, and do not sin." Ephesians 6:26 (NKJ)

Perhaps it's because our feelings and actions are entirely different.

FEELINGS ARE SIMPLY MARKERS THAT LET US KNOW WHAT'S GOING ON INSIDE OF US.

SIGNALS + TRIGGERS

When I got married, I didn't realize there were two types of people on Earth. Those that knew how much gas is in their car and those who simply knew they needed gas when the light came on. I married a man who knew exactly how much fuel was in the car and I was the "light watcher."

My feelings are like a dashboard. They allow me to understand what is going on inside my soul. My emotions tell me if something needs attention. The lights in each of our vehicles trigger us, showing us what's going on under the hood. They allow us to see things that need our attention that we would never have seen before.

RESPECT + DISRESPECT

If someone does not allow you to feel a specific way, they are being disrespectful to you. They can disagree with you or even hate that you feel that way, but they don't get to violate your autonomy. They don't get to dictate how you feel, no matter how powerful they may believe they are.

Once you have a feeling, you get to choose how you will interpret it.

Am I going to feel disrespected?

Am I going to choose to feel hurt?

Have I chosen to interpret that emotion with empathy?

A plethora of feelings come to me every day, but I have the power of choice. I get to choose whatever feelings I want to stay. I must understand that no one can make me feel a specific way.

No one can make me feel powerless.

No one can make me feel helpless.

No one can make me angry.

No one is that powerful.

I am powerful enough to choose my feelings. They are mine and mine alone, and they are to be respected. No one is powerful enough, even though they may think they are, to go inside my yard and make me choose to feel a specific way. Likewise, I cannot go into anyone else's yard and choose for them. I'm not that powerful.

Someone may say to you, "*You made me angry!*" That is not the truth. "*I can't go inside your yard and choose anger for you. You did that.*" Irresponsible people would love nothing more than for you to feel responsible for their feelings. We'll talk more about this later.

HEALTHY FEELINGS

Just because I feel something doesn't mean I have to act on it. If I can feel something without immediately putting it into action, it's a great sign of maturity. I'm a Spirit-led person when I allow my spirit to lead me and not be led by my emotions. My feelings are in my yard, but they aren't ruling my property. They are signaling what needs attention without dictating it.

REME MBER

+ God isn't neutral about our feelings. He endorses them.

+ Jesus, who was fully God and fully man, had emotions just like us.

+ Feelings are simply markers that let us know what's going on inside of us.

+ My feelings are in MY yard.

+ I am powerful enough to choose my feelings. They are mine and mine alone, and they are to be respected.

+ No one has the power to reach into my yard and make me choose my feelings.

+ Just because I feel something doesn't mean I have to act on it.

If you have allowed others to dictate your feelings, it's time to take your power back. I love what the Bible says in Philippians 4 in the Amplified Version.

"I can do all things [which He has called me to do] through Him who strengthens **and** empowers me [to fulfill His purpose—I am self-sufficient in Christ's sufficiency; I am ready for anything and equal to anything through Him who infuses me with inner strength and confident peace.]" - Philippians 4:13

Let's break this down - LOOK AT THIS TRUTH!

I CAN	HE CAN
I can do all things through Christ.	He can call me to do them.
I can live a powerful life.	He can empower me.
I can live in strength.	He can infuse me with inner strength.
I can live sufficiently.	He can be my sufficiency.
I can be ready for anything.	He can empower me to fulfull my purpose.
I can be equal to anything.	He can infuse me with confident peace.

I want you to say this aloud, *"No one is powerful enough to make me feel any specific way. I'm getting my power back! If I want to be sad and feel mad, that is about me. I understand now and own it. No one can make me feel hurt. Yes, they can hurt me, and hurt might be my initial feeling, but I can choose to feel a different way about it in the end."*

RESPOND

Here's a quick FEELING CHEAT SHEET. Feelings are important to God.

Let's take a moment to identify what emotions you have today.

5 STEP FEELING CHEATSHEET

1. What is the emotion I'm feeling? (circle one or more)

+ Anger [mad]

+ Anxious [Fear of losing something or not having enough]

+ Shame

+ Sadness [sad]

+ Fear [scared]

+ Guilt

+ _____

+ _____

2. **My feelings are here to show me something.**
What are my emotions trying to tell me?
(circle one or more)

+ I feel disappointed

+ I feel anxious

+ I feel excited

+ _____

+ _____

+ _____

3. **Identify where I might have felt this before:**

_____

_____

_____

4. **Identify the behavior it's producing in me:**

_____

_____

_____

5. **Would I like to reframe this feeling around truth?**
What would that sound like if I changed my feeling?

_____

_____

TAKEAWAYS

+ HEALTHY BOUNDARIES ARE FENCES, NOT WALLS.

They aren't barriers we've constructed to make our lives a fortress, a place where no one comes in and no one goes out. Boundaries keep our connections strong. They help us protect love by taking ownership and responsibility.

+ I'M 100% THE OWNER OF MY YARD, WHICH MEANS I HAVE 100% AUTHORITY AND ANOINTING OVER MY PROPERTY.

My yard has an invisible gate around it and within it lies the things God holds me personally responsible for. When I get to heaven, God will ask me how I stewarded these specific areas.

+ PART OF MY STEWARDSHIP AND OWNERSHIP IS MY PHYSICAL BODY.

When it comes to living a healthy life, which **Ephesians 1:4** tells us we are called to do, we must understand this includes our whole being. Your body is valuable to God because it houses Him and, therefore, the way you care for and protect it matters to God. He views your body as a place of holiness.

✛ MY SOUL IS THE PLACE WHERE REGENERATION TAKES PLACE.

When Christ comes to live inside of me, my spirit becomes "born-again." At once! It doesn't need to be regenerated because it is brand new and works perfectly.

✛ NO ONE HAS THE POWER TO REACH INTO MY YARD AND MAKE ME CHOOSE MY FEELINGS.

My emotions are mine and mine alone. No one is powerful enough, even though they may think they are, to go inside my yard and make me choose to feel a specific way. Likewise, I cannot go into anyone else's yard and choose for them. I'm not that powerful.

FIND I DO BOUNDARIES STUDY VIDEOS ALONG WITH OTHER RESOURCES AT TRUTHTOTABLE.COM

CONFIDENCE

"THINGS I DO NOT OWN"

Welcome to Week Three!

I trust you learned all about what's in your yard!

Week Three is all about the transformation of releasing shame and blame, the power of God in our everyday life, and what it really takes to break out of fear and confusion.

Let's get started!

DAY ELEVEN

WHY AM I THINKING ABOUT THIS?

"Attitude is a little thing that makes a big difference."
- Winston Churchill

Your soul has three specific areas of stewardship.

Yesterday, we learned that our **feelings** are entirely in our yards. We are allowed to feel our deepest feelings and they inherently have no moral value. Our emotions are given by God to help reveal the deepest areas of our belief system. We are anointed to accept, interpret, and eventually decide which feelings to resist or accept.

The second area of ownership is my **attitude**.

My attitude is in my yard; it's mine and I own it. Attitudes come from various places, but primarily they come from my values and belief systems, and usually from the places and people I grew up around. Attitudes are often village-based. By that I mean, *"I think this way because everyone else around me thinks this way and, if I want to belong, I need to think this way too."*

Jeremiah calls the people of God out about this precise attitude in chapter 22.

"I spoke to you in your [times of] prosperity, but you said, I will not listen! This has been your attitude from your youth; you have not obeyed My voice."
Jeremiah 22:21 AMP

IF FEELINGS ARE HOW I FEEL ABOUT LIFE, THEN MY ATTITUDES ARE WHAT I THINK ABOUT LIFE.

MY THOUGHT LIFE IS HOW I TALK TO MYSELF EVERY DAY.

My thought life is how I talk to myself every day. Whatever I believe and value will eventually seep into my attitudes and feelings. It's important I don't try to change my attitudes by mimicking the outward actions of others. Instead, I need to continually evaluate my belief systems and values because they will eventually change the way I think about life... resulting in new attitudes; resulting in transformation.

ANXIOUS THOUGHTS

Anxious thoughts plagued my mind.

Thoughts like, *"What if they found out about my schedule and that I could actually pull it off? What if they decided I could do what they were asking?"*

"What if they found out and decided I was mean ... or lazy or just plain selfish?"

"What if they thought I was avoiding work or avoiding them?" or worse, *"They decided I was a terrible person, and didn't care about anyone but myself."*

I was none of these things.

I was a 27-year-old woman who had successfully navigated a productive life. I gave my life to Christ at the age of 17, and worked hard to build His church.

I was the girl who could DO IT ALL and, by that, I mean "I DID IT ALL."

As a family, we started a church when I was 19. I answered phones, planned events, and helped develop an Internship Program. Eventually, taking the role of a worship pastor, I served for eight years in that position. When that wasn't enough, knowing I had the heart to speak, I became a teaching pastor. I spent 40 to 60 hours a week cultivating this gift.

It's embarrassing to say, but I felt like God's favorite girl when I worked that hard for Him. I felt worthy of the calling He had given me.

But now, as a new mom and a new wife, I couldn't do everything I'd done before.

I was struggling. Desperately trying to do everything and, yet, unknowingly, I was fighting to be worthy. Frantic to be that girl God could depend on, yet fumbling the ball. Dropping my responsibilities and letting people down. The harder I tried, the more I felt like I couldn't get it together. I was disintegrating into a "burned-out believer."

The moment I learned that other people's thoughts were not in my yard, and that I was not responsible for what they thought about me, I was free.

Okay, it wasn't that simple.

It took time to unpack this toxic way of thinking.

Growing up, I was raised to believe I could change other people's thoughts. I was that powerful. I'd also been taught if I did all the right things in the right way, I was powerful enough to alter what people thought about me.

This belief gave me a false sense of power.

But when I couldn't keep it together and I couldn't do the things that made other people think good thoughts about me, I panicked.

Obsessed with what other people would think, I was terrified to communicate something they potentially would disagree with. After all, I was that powerful!

One morning, in group counseling, we began to practice what it would look like to give back other people's thoughts.

"Ok," the group leader began. *"Havilah, tell me what you're struggling with."*

I quickly rattled off all the thoughts I seemingly knew others were thinking about me.

She cut me off.

"No, you are not that powerful! Why do you believe they are thinking that?" I responded, *"Well, it's just that if I say 'No' to them, then they will think I'm lazy or selfish or entitled."*

She interjected again. *"Yes, they may think those thoughts. But they may also think something entirely different. They may think that you are a new mom and wife and that you're learning. Regardless, it doesn't really matter because their thoughts are not in your yard, and you are not powerful enough to change what they believe or think about you. It's a waste of time and energy. It's only going to hurt your ability to protect what matters most to you."*

I had never thought of it like that before.

As the words left her mouth, it felt like someone was in my mind shoveling all the clutter, thoughts, and burdens I'd been carrying around.

EDITING YOUR THOUGHTS

Let this sink in:

HOW OTHER PEOPLE CHOOSE TO RESPOND SAYS EVERYTHING ABOUT THEM, BUT HOW YOU CHOOSE TO RESPOND SAYS EVERYTHING ABOUT YOU.

It will ALWAYS be about them.

They choose those thoughts, just like they choose those feelings.

Here's what a healthy thought narrative sounds like:

"I'm not in charge of what other people think about me. The only thing I know is what they are willing to communicate with me. If they are unhappy about something, then they have decided to be unhappy. My response to every action is not powerful enough to change their response or reaction. If they are happy that I said 'yes,' then they have decided they will be happy. If they are unhappy that I have said 'no,' that is their decision. All of this is in their yard. I am not powerful enough to make them feel good or bad about my decisions. I'm only powerful enough to own my thoughts, feelings, and actions. Period."

When I put my thoughts in the proper yard, I take my power back. If I believe you control what I think, then I have given you too much power. If I believe your actions dictate what I think about you, I'm too powerful in my own eyes.

It's a false sense of control.

I am not that powerful.

Neither are you.

Once we get clear on who owns what - we can get busy renewing our minds to have the most prosperous thought life, resulting in a healthy and Godly belief system. **My belief system will directly connect to my values, and my attitude will align with my vision.**

Paul encouraged us to have a fresh, spiritual attitude.

"And be constantly renewed in the spirit of your mind [having a fresh mental and spiritual attitude]," Ephesians 4:23

REME MBER

Wow... this inspires me! The Holy Spirit wants to help us have the attitude that enables us to prosper and grow. The Word of God helps us understand what Godly attitudes look like and how to keep them growing in our lives.

+ Attitudes come from various places, but primarily they come from my values and belief systems.

+ If feelings are how I feel about life, then my attitudes are what I think about life.

+ How other people choose to respond says everything about them. How I choose to respond says everything about me.

+ When I place thoughts in the proper yard, I take my power back.

+ My belief system will directly connect to my values, and my attitude will align with my vision.

+ The Holy Spirit wants to help me have the attitude that enables me to prosper and grow. The Word of God helps me understand what a Godly attitude looks like and how to keep it growing in my life.

READ

" For I know the plans and thoughts that I have for you,' says the Lord, 'plans for peace and well-being and not for disaster, to give you a future and a hope." Jeremiah 29:11 (AMP)

God has the most incredible thoughts about me! His attitude about me aligns with His beliefs about me.

I have the highest value to Him because my worth is not based on what's growing in my yard, but on the price He paid to redeem me. God sent His only Son to die for me before I could ever do one thing for Him. My value will always be in my God-given position. My position as a child of God came well before my behavior to please Him.

Whatever we allow to grow in our yard (even if it's obeying God) will never add greater value to our life. It will only add enjoyment to our life and make us more useful in God's Kingdom.

Think about this statement for a moment.

God is not uneven in His parenting and always sees me as:

Loveable

Valuable

Forgivable

Changeable

And there's NOTHING I can do to change this.

Simply said, *it's my job to agree with God.*

RESPOND

5-MINUTE MIND RENEWAL EXERCISE

Today, I want to encourage you to spend some time renewing your mind. Remember, if we know the truth, the truth will set us free. (See John 8:32)

Take a moment to consider the following statements and characteristics God sees you as:

+ **I AM Loveable**

+ **I AM Valuable**

+ **I AM Forgivable**

+ **I AM Changeable**

And there's NOTHING I can do to change this.

Which of the above do you struggle with believing the most? (Circle one or more)

Now, let's do a little research* on the word(s) you circled and discover the truth according to the Bible. I recommend you word search or google to help you research what the Bible says.

Now write it down.

What scripture(s) did you find that speaks to this truth?

---

*I recommend two different free websites to help you do your research. www.youversion.com & www.biblegateway.com

WHY AM I DOING THIS AGAIN?

I grew up believing there was the perfect person for me and my job was to find him. I'm not sure if living through the 1990s when romantic comedies were at an all-time high helped. Movies like, *"You've Got Mail," "Sleepless in Seattle," "Ever After,"* and *"While You Were Sleeping,"* to name a few, indoctrinated our generation.

Church life wasn't much help, either.

The Biblical picture of Eve having been created for Adam and Jacob finding Rebekah helped to confirm this theology. I needed to find the perfect person in order to be smack dab in the will of God. Finding that human was my ultimate goal.

Thoughts like, *"What if I don't like the one God prepared for me?"* or *"What if I never find that person?"* seemed to plague my heavenly "arranged marriage." Throw in the occasional testimony of *"God gave me a dream"* and *"We are made for each other,"* and the theory was concrete.

When you're young and naïve, even idealistic, this sounds perfect. It's a quest to find the ideal person — the Prince Charming in my Cinderella story.

I spent years saying "No" to various suitors, believing they weren't my prince. But the older I got, the more I became concerned that my Prince Charming wasn't coming. *Perhaps he lost his GPS. Did he marry the wrong person?* I couldn't even go there - it was a devastating thought.

When my husband, Ben, and I started dating, we had such a great relationship. But after some time, I became convinced he wasn't the one. After all, God hadn't spoken to me. I didn't have a prophetic dream or a supernatural confirmation from Heaven - radio silence.

I was ready to let him go, but I felt the Lord begin to challenge me.

God started to poke holes in my belief system.

Beginning with, *"If there's only one person for you, then what about those who remarry?"* or *"Could they have chosen the wrong person?"* *"Did they mess up the whole romantic universe because someone got impatient and married the closest thing they could find?"*

I'll never forget God speaking to me.

"Havilah, I'm not going to make that decision for you. If you love him, and he loves Me, and you enjoy doing life together, then you are welcome to make that decision, and I'll bless it." I was stunned. The God of the Universe was leaving the decision up to me? An overwhelming possibility.

But I followed my peace. I had chosen Ben, and he had chosen me to be his life partner. We were completely sober, eyes wide open, when we made this powerful decision.

I wouldn't know the impact of my choice for years.

How incredibly important this exchange with God would be. Knowing I had been fully awake to the decision of marrying Ben kept my feet grounded. I had made the decision and the choice was 100% mine.

It wasn't until a very critical time in our marriage did this become glaringly clear why God had allowed this. Through tears, I asked God why he had me marry Ben. To which He replied, *"That was your decision."*

"Wait... what?" I answered. *"Why did you make it entirely my decision?"* He responded, *"Because, if it was 100% your decision, then you get to stay powerful in the relationship. The CHOICE is the thing that keeps you powerful."*

THE POWER OF CHOICE

The third and final area in my yard are my **CHOICES.**

God holds me entirely responsible for every decision I make. My choices are solely mine. As an adult, what I choose to do is always within my power.

**GOD NEVER INVADES OUR
PERSONAL CHOICE OR WILL.**

He initiates. He knocks (Rev. 3:20). He speaks the truth and then leaves it up to me to make the decision.

Think about Adam and Eve in the Garden of Eden, with the Tree of the Knowledge of Good and Evil. A clear example of how God used boundaries, limits without control, and the power of choice.

God clearly outlined to Adam and Eve they could have anything in the whole garden except that fruit. Adam and Eve used their freedom and free will. Knowing the eternal impact of their choice, God did not strike them with lightning when they ate *(Lord knows, I'd be handing out heavenly spankings.)* God didn't interrupt them in the middle of making their devastating decision. He simply said, ***"If you eat of this tree, there will be consequences."***

When God finally found them hiding in the garden, He asked them questions that revealed their heart. Even though their choices rocked them, God continued with His boundary. He cast them out of the garden, the consequence for their sin.

Reminded once again,

WE WILL ALWAYS HAVE THE POWER TO MAKE OUR CHOICES, BUT WE DO NOT GET TO CHOOSE OUR CONSEQUENCES.

GETTING MY POWER BACK

I'm the first one to blame someone else for my choices. After all, if they had done the right thing or thought of everything, I wouldn't be in this predicament. My default is to blame someone else. It's ugly but honest.

I never saw blame as the very thing that was taking my power away. I had placed my *feelings, attitudes,* and *choices* in someone else's yard; I gave my power away. I may have felt free from responsibility but whatever they chose to do now dictated my life.

I would feel sorry for myself. I might even be angry. But I didn't see my responsibility in the predicament, because I'd given my power away.

I'll never forget the time I was telling my counselor about my husband's driving. It seemed to be an endless place of contention. Getting in the car meant we would scrimmage all the way to the next destination. He tailgated, I yelled. It always escalated to me going silent and him getting angry.

I told my counselor how upset I was about it. Ben needed to change. To which she replied, *"Well, then, why do you*

WE WILL ALWAYS HAVE THE POWER TO MAKE OUR CHOICES, BUT WE DO NOT GET TO CHOOSE OUR CONSEQUENCES.

ride with him? If it makes you anxious, and he isn't willing to change after you've asked, then why are you giving him that responsibility?"

Immediately, I was defensive. *"Well, isn't it disrespectful not to ride with your spouse? I mean, doesn't it just look like I'm throwing a fit and manipulating him?"* Her turn, *"You were the one that just told me his driving made you feel unsafe and when you asked him to stop driving like that, he wasn't willing to change."*

I had NEVER thought of it like that before.

I was willing to be the 7-year-old little girl in the front seat, throwing a tantrum. I wailed. Begged. Pleaded. But I did not own my choice, which was hiding under the "good Christian wife blanket." From that day forward, I never saw myself as a powerless person in the front seat of a car. Once I was willing to communicate and follow-through, I got my power back. *We'll talk more about this in the next chapter.*

HOW DO WE TAKE OWNERSHIP OF OUR YARD?

I need to take 100% responsibility for my choices.

I cannot blame my actions on anyone else other than myself. If they are behaving poorly, guess what? Their choice to behave poorly is in their yard and they are the owner, even if they don't want to admit it.

Yes, other people's choices affect my life.

Sometimes it can bring devastating consequences, just like Adam and Eve's choices. But in the face of catastrophic loss, the ONLY WAY TO GET MY POWER BACK is to take my portion, whether it's a small sliver or a massive log, as the rightful owner. Only then can I receive FULL grace and wisdom to make the next choice.

God holds me responsible for each choice I make. God chooses the consequences of my actions, but ultimately my actions are in my yard. I can no longer look at the person next to me, blaming them for the decisions I've made. It's a false sense of freedom.

Lastly, my spouse is not responsible for my choices.

I know. *You were wondering how you can live with someone who is behaving poorly? What do you do to get them to take responsibility for their actions?*

Here's the secret... Are you ready?

Lean in.

You CAN'T make anyone do anything!!! Remember, you are not that powerful. You are only powerful enough to make your next choice. Own your next attitude and interpret your next feeling.

Stewarding my yard will give me plenty to do! If I manage my boundaries well, I will have very little time for anything else. It will take almost 100% of my attention to focus on what my feelings are revealing, what thoughts are creating my attitudes, and what choices I need to own.

Maintaining my yard is a full-time job, and that's a good thing!

Sustaining healthy boundaries requires me to stay fully awake in my daily life. It will take enormous energy to recognize negative feelings that want to take root and poison my heart. It will require a relentless spirit to reevaluate my attitudes. To venture deep into my values and belief system to root out an unbelieving or critical spirit. It will require me to function as a *spiritual adult.* Understanding that all of my choices, whether past, present, or future, are mine. I own them, and I will reap the fruit of them.

REME MBER

+ The third and final area in my yard is my CHOICES.

+ God never invades my personal choice or will.

+ I will always have the power to make my choices, but I do not get to choose my consequences.

+ I need to take 100% responsibility for my choices.

+ Stewarding my yard will give me plenty to do! If I manage my boundaries well, I will have very little time for anything else.

+ Sustaining healthy boundaries requires me to stay fully awake in my daily life.

"But I need something more! For if I know the law but still can't keep it, and if the power of sin within me keeps sabotaging my best intentions, I obviously need help! I realize that I don't have what it takes. I can will it, but I can't do it. I decide to do good, but I don't really do it; I decide not to do bad, but then I do it anyway. My decisions, such as they are, don't result in actions. Something has gone wrong deep within me and gets the better of me every time."
Romans 7:17-20 (Message)

When we talk about choices, we can often feel ashamed because we've made poor choices in the past. We may even be living with some of those consequences. The enemy of our soul would love for us to live deeply discouraged. He wants us to believe that we don't have what it takes to create and live a healthy life. He is the "father of lies" **(John 8:44).**

Don't be discouraged! We are looking for a spiritual breakthrough to help us do what we can't do for ourselves. When we get trapped in addiction, codependency, negative thinking, and poor lifestyle choices, we live utterly defeated. Like the above scripture says, "**I can will it, but I can't do it.**"

Listen - If I could do it ALL on my own, I wouldn't need a Savior.

Read this last paragraph of **Romans 7**...

> **"The answer, thank God, is that Jesus Christ can and does. He acted to set things right in this life of contradictions where I want to serve God with all my heart and mind, but am pulled by the influence of sin to do something totally different."**

Our hope is in Jesus! Jesus came to do what we could not do for ourselves.

RESPOND

Take a moment and talk to God. If you can, pray this aloud:

"Lord, I look to You. I need your help today. My life can seem overwhelming without Your wisdom to know what needs to be there, and what doesn't. I ask You for supernatural discernment to understand where my property lines begin and where they end. I ask You to empower me to do the right thing; to give others back their feelings, attitudes, and choices. Likewise, to take mine back in ownership and steward them well. I ask for wisdom to see where my belief systems have led me to cling to attitudes that are harming me. I want to change!

I ask You to help me. Help me show up as the spiritual grown-up you've made me. I want to own my choices for what they are. I will no longer render myself as powerless in the midst of my daily living! I accept the Holy Spirit's empowerment.

Strength to live the life I'm called to live, with Godly boundaries, and a well-managed yard.

I pray this in Jesus' name! Amen."

HOW DO I TELL PEOPLE WHAT I NEED?

One of the greatest struggles in my Christian life has been accepting that others want to put their feelings, attitudes, and choices in my yard. They see nothing wrong with expecting me to take care of them. They believe I am responsible for managing their feelings, putting up with their attitudes, and having insight into their choices.

It's easy for them to see me as responsible, because I am a reliable person. If you can relate with this, it will require working with the Holy Spirit to maintain healthy boundaries.

IRRESPONSIBLE PEOPLE LOVE TO TAKE ADVANTAGE OF RESPONSIBLE PEOPLE.

It's not always malicious. It's trained behavior that has worked for them, and it's *kind of genius!*

The other day, my son came home from middle school. As he pushed through the front door, wordlessly passing by me, I called out, *"Hey! How was your day? Did you have a good day?"* His response? An irritated grunt.

I persisted. *"Hey, did you have a good or a bad day? Can you give your Mom one or two sentences?"* His face said it all. He turned to me and angrily answered, *"I'm too tired to talk! I'm exhausted. Why do you always have to ask me questions? Why do you always want me to do something? I don't want to talk to you right now."*

Tempted to punish him for his rudeness, I stopped myself, quickly noting his response. I planned out how I would communicate my limits. I smiled and kept going throughout my day.

About an hour later, as I'm standing in the kitchen, he enters with an excited look on his face. He was working on a project and needed a ski mask that was stored way up in the garage. He needed my help. To which I replied, *"I'm too tired to talk! I'm exhausted. Why do you always have to ask me questions? Why do you always want me to do something? I don't want to talk to you right now."*

Our eyes met, and a huge smile came across his face.

He knew exactly what I was doing. I quickly explained that I was not comfortable with his disrespect. It was a perfect example for him to get the picture.

COMMUNICATING BOUNDARIES

Irresponsible people NEVER learn through lectures. They only learn through consequences. You can lecture all you want about them taking responsibility, but nothing will change unless you are willing to put your money where your mouth is and remove your help.

It's easy to think, *"Isn't that mean? Didn't Jesus want us to help others?"* Remember the difference between a backpack and a boulder?

Yelling at someone to grab their backpack will NEVER work.

Handing them the backpack, walking away, and refusing to carry it is the only way forward. I promise you, irresponsible people will try to get you to pick it up again.

They may bait you by attacking your character *(let's be honest...responsible people rely heavily on their reputation. That's why they are so reliable.)* They may try to throw it back at you, hoping you won't be able to take the pressure. *After all, if they don't do it, then who is going to do it?*

That is not your responsibility.

What if, instead of me feeling bad about it, I reframed it as living more obediently to God? It would sound something like, **"I've decided that for me to be more obedient to God, I am no longer willing to carry this for you."**

When you start to feel afraid that they may be mad at you or believe you're a terrible person, you will have to talk to yourself. Tell yourself, **"I cannot make anyone feel anything. I am not that powerful,"** and, **"I have done nothing wrong. I am not in trouble. This is only anxiety the enemy is trying to put on me."**

Once you understand that other people would love you to carry their loads, you will be able to discern when the enemy is trying to burden you with things that God has not asked you to carry.

Part of executing healthy boundaries is communicating them well. It doesn't help me at all if I have boundaries, but I never share them. I set myself up to be violated, disregarded, hurt, or disappointed with someone who may have absolutely no idea of the consequence of their actions.

Newsflash - people can't read your mind!

Critical words, passive-aggressive behavior, body language, and sarcasm are all *hostile communication.* They don't foster healthy relationships and they don't build trust.

HOW WE COMMUNICATE OUR BOUNDARIES IS JUST AS IMPORTANT AS HAVING THEM.

HOW WE COMMUNICATE OUR BOUNDARIES IS JUST AS IMPORTANT AS HAVING THEM.

Some of us don't like to set boundaries because we've only experienced people being mean, or even cruel, when communicating their limits. My yelling, *"Don't do that!,"* *"Stop touching me,"* or *" Leave me alone,"* isn't communicating boundaries. All I'm doing is shouting demands.

The art of communicating healthy boundaries is saying words in the kindest way possible. You don't have to rely on anger, aggression, or avoidance in order to feel powerful. Be confident in knowing what you own, and you will be able to communicate boundaries without fear.

It's possible to get so skilled at this type of communication that those you're communicating with won't even know what hit them. They will see you as respectful, powerful, and confident because you know what you want and how to communicate it. They will want to be around you because they can trust you. You say what you mean and mean what you say. You don't play games! You show up like the spiritual grown-up that you are. Remember, even if they don't like it, "You're not powerful enough to make them *perceive* anything." *Wink.*

One of the best tools I've learned in communicating boundaries is to try and communicate with a short repeatable sentence. I like to start my sentences with, *"I'm crystal clear ..."* or *"I've decided..."* It leaves no room for confusion. Second, I repeat what I said the first time as many times as necessary.

If you're communicating a boundary and the person you're talking to doesn't hear you, simply repeat the same thing.

EXAMPLE: *"I'm crystal clear that I won't be able to help you with your event. In an effort to be more obedient to God, I'm going to need to decline your invitation. Thank you again!"*

RESPONSE: *"I **thought** you said you could do it. We were really expecting you to help us since you **never** help us with anything else. I have **no other options** but you."*

Ok, look at this response.

First, an assumption - *"I thought you said you could."*

Second, extreme wording - *"never"* or *"always," "every time," "all the time,"* etc.

Third, fatal wording - *"I have no other options."*

All of these things are meant to draw you in and make you change your mind. So, the best response is your first response. Repeat the exact same thing without using more words or being triggered to change your mind. And remember,

---

THEY DON'T HAVE TO LIKE YOUR RESPONSE FOR IT TO BE THE RIGHT RESPONSE FOR YOU.

What happens if I communicate my boundaries, but the person I'm sharing with always talks me out of them?

If I'm having a hard time sticking with my decision, then they've reached the little boy or little girl on the inside of me—the one who doesn't feel like a grown-up. They've taken control of my yard and I'm now a hostage.

The goal isn't for everyone to agree with my boundaries. The goal isn't even to say it flawlessly. The goal is to share them without altering the decision I made beforehand. It's okay for me to change my mind. Adults change their minds all the time. But I need to be honest with myself and answer this question: **Was I in charge of myself the whole time? Did I do what I set out to do?**

Another way to identify powerlessness in my mind is to question all of my "have to's." The words "have to" is the language of a *victim mentality*. As an adult, there are things I need to do, but there is a big difference between my "have to's" versus my "need to's" or " get to's." **The wording isn't the point; my perspective is the point.** My words frame my belief system. If I can reframe the feeling of no longer being a victim to feelings, attitudes, and choices of others, I can discover my power. Only then can I be fully present with the power I possess.

Let's read about a rich young ruler who came asking Jesus a question.

Turn your Bibles to **Matthew 10:17-27** and read the story.

We see Jesus tells the rich young ruler the hard truth and sets a firm boundary. He says, **"Sell all you have and give to the poor, and you will have a treasure in Heaven."**

Jesus sets a boundary.

He communicates very clearly what the young man would need to do in order to have what he wanted. The rich young ruler was not willing to do what Jesus asked. The Bible says, **"...he went away sad, because he had great wealth."**

Let me ask you a few questions:

Did Jesus initiate the conversation?

Did Jesus ask the young man to do something only he could do?

When the man walked away sad, did Jesus run after him?

Did Jesus interrupt His command to make the young man happy?

All of these answers have a resounding..."No!"

Jesus communicated a boundary and followed through, essentially protecting His Kingdom. Many of us expect God to interrupt His commands to keep us happy.

Was the rich young ruler powerless?

Absolutely not!

He had every right to make any decision he wanted, but he likewise had to accept what Jesus said. Jesus was not going to break His property lines to keep the man happy. We see this throughout the entire Bible.

As children, we are not always responsible for our choices, attitudes, or feelings, but we are as adults. As the Bible challenges each of us, "**Choose this day whom you will serve.**" I believe it is that simple.

Are you committed to managing your choices, feelings, and attitudes in such a way that pleases God and demonstrates a manageable, peaceful, and love-filled life?

REME MBER

If you want to be more like God, then establish and communicate healthy boundaries in your life. Communicate them clearly and kindly.

+ Irresponsible people love to take advantage of responsible people.

+ It will require working with the Holy Spirit to maintain healthy boundaries.

+ Irresponsible people NEVER learn through lectures. They only learn through consequences.

+ Part of executing healthy boundaries is communicating them well.

+ Others don't have to like my response for it to be the right response.

+ The goal isn't for everyone to agree with my boundaries. The goal is to share them without altering the decision I made beforehand.

BY HAVILAH CUNNINGTON

Hurry with your answer, God! I'm nearly at the end of my rope. Don't turn away; don't ignore me! That would be certain death. If you wake me each morning with the sound of your loving voice, I'll go to sleep each night trusting in you. Point out the road I must travel; I'm all ears, all eyes before you. Save me from my enemies, God— you're my only hope! Teach me how to live to please you, because you're my God. Lead me by your blessed Spirit into cleared and level pastureland.
Psalm 143:7-10

It's best not to verbally shove everyone's attitudes, feelings, and choices back into their yard. But rather privately and prayerfully ask the Holy Spirit to help you firmly and gently keep your boundaries clear.

Your motivation should always be one of obedience. Set your heart on the truth that God created boundaries to keep you safe and your life more manageable. You were not designed to live without boundaries, and if you try, it will eventually hurt you.

Likewise, you need to see that having a lack of boundaries is disobedient and harmful to your spiritual life and relationships. Like the Psalmist said, **"Teach me how to live to please you, because you're my God."** You will need God's help to show you how to live.

RESPOND

Today, it's important to see God as a good Father, not a controlling Master. Understanding He has boundaries and limits is part of His commitment to keeping us safe. If He allowed everything, all of the time, and never followed through with what He said, we would all be in big trouble. It is His kindness and love that sets boundaries.

Like the Psalmist, let's take a moment and write out a prayer asking God to help you. You may have never thought of asking Him to help you. He's an ever-present God, ready and willing to come to your aid...anytime.

You don't have to do this alone.

HOW DO I MAKE GOOD FRIENDS?

"YOU TRY TO DO THE THINGS
EVEN I DON'T TRY TO DO." - GOD

We all have a lot of questions on boundaries when it comes to relationships. Boundaries would be so much easier if they only had to do with ourselves, but because we live on Earth with other humans, understanding how we relate to others really matters.

I once had an intern who was vibrant, energetic, and entertaining. From the moment we met, she was dynamic and magnetic. She was special. Within weeks, she had migrated into each of our lives. Her confidence created a sense of belief that she was 'one of us.'

But as the weeks turned to months, I started feeling an uneasiness about her. I couldn't put my finger on it. I just knew the more I was around her, the more I wanted to keep my inner world from her. I slowly began withholding things from her and consciously creating privacy.

One day, when I needed to give her some insight because her actions had resulted in less than desirable consequences that left me and my staff picking up some of the pieces, she resisted. Having invested hours in our relationship, we didn't want to give up that quickly so we continued to pursue the relationship. We loved her, but she decided she didn't want to receive our advice or have anything to do with us.

She pulled away entirely, abandoning the internship, leaving as fast as she had come. We were left feeling a whirlwind of emotions. An awkward sadness, but also a sense of embarrassment. We had opened our world to her, but all she did was walk in, take what she could, and leave in a very immature way. We had shared many private dimensions of our lives, thoughts reserved for deep friendships, and we couldn't get them back.

I ran into her years later. The interaction was brief and kind. But, as I climbed into my car, I couldn't help but feel a vulnerability in seeing her again. I'd let her in too fast and too far. I had learned a hard lesson — one about friendship and boundaries.

Jesus loved everyone while on Earth.

There wasn't a person He didn't extend love, compassion, and dignity to. But Jesus, being fully God and fully man, had limitations. He wasn't able to offer Himself, all of the time, to anyone who needed Him. The needs of others didn't dictate His exposure to them. His life wasn't accessible to everyone; that would not have been possible or appropriate.

We see through Scripture that Jesus limited His exposure to others by varying degrees. Jesus operated with boundaries. All of His relationships had different levels of access.

Relational spheres are places others have access to.

Initially, Jesus called the twelve disciples to come and follow Him **(Matthew 10:1-15).** This was the first time Scripture mentions Him initiating relationships. These twelve men would be with Jesus for the next three years: eating, fellowshipping, learning, being equipped and equipping others. Essentially, these men became His world-class leadership team. They also became Jesus' close relational community.

The Bible clearly implies that three men — Peter, James, and John — had an even closer connection to Jesus and greater access to Him. They were the core group inside the twelve. Jesus allowed these three to be with Him during some of the most intimate and personal experiences of His life. Jesus specifically brought only these three men along with Him to Jarius' house, where He raised his daughter from the dead. *"He allowed no one to go with Him but Peter and James and John."* (Mark 5:37) It wasn't a coincidence these three alone were with Jesus; it was His clear decision to bring them and not others. They alone had access to monumental moments like the transfiguration when Moses and Elijah met Jesus on the mountaintop (Matthew 17:1-8), and the Garden of Gethsemane, when Jesus called out to His Father before His crucifixion (Matthew 26:36-38).

Jesus even seemed to have a best friend among the three. John referred to himself as "the one Jesus loved" (John 14:13). John wasn't boasting when he wrote this. He was acknowledging a premeditated placement Jesus intended. John was there for Jesus in the Garden of Gethsemane and the only one of the 12 at the foot of the Cross.

"While the soldiers were looking after themselves, Jesus' mother, his aunt, Mary the wife of Clopas, and Mary Magdalene stood at the foot of the cross. Jesus saw his mother and the disciple he loved standing near her. He said to his mother, 'Woman, here is your son.' Then to the disciple, 'Here is your mother.' From that moment the disciple accepted her as his own mother."
John 19:26-27

Yet, even Christ's closest disciple didn't have unlimited access to Him. Jesus would spend quality time alone, cultivating an intimate relationship with His Heavenly Father. **(Luke 4:1-2, 14-15) He didn't sacrifice His own spiritual needs in order to maintain healthy relationships with others.**

Beyond the twelve, other disciples had access to Jesus on a regular basis. In time, He sent out an additional group of 72 followers **(Luke 10:1-12)**. These 72 disciples had learned how to minister by following Jesus, up close and personal. But these 72 didn't have the same level of access to Jesus as the twelve. Likewise, the twelve didn't have the depth of connection to Jesus as the three. And the three were not as close as John.

When we put everyone on the same relational level, we can get in trouble. It can lead to burnout, misunderstandings, and hurt feelings.

WE WERE NOT CREATED TO BRING EVERYBODY INTO OUR INNER WORLD. JESUS DEMONSTRATED THIS BY HOW HE LIVED. THE BIBLE SAYS THAT JESUS TAUGHT NOTHING IN PRIVATE THAT HE WOULDN'T SAY IN PUBLIC (JOHN 18:20). BUT, IT DOESN'T SAY HE SHARED EVERY PERSONAL DIMENSION OF HIS THOUGHTS AND FEELINGS WITH EVERYONE AROUND HIM.

Let's do a quick review.

RELATIONAL SPHERES

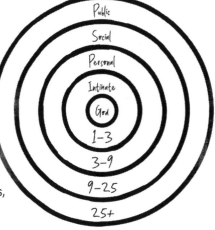

LEVEL 1 - GOD SPOT

+ Space for 1

+ Deepest Core

+ Sacred Space

+ Heart, Thoughts, Emotions, Longings, Plans, Pain, Etc.

+ Jesus + Father in Heaven

LEVEL 2 - INTIMATE

+ Space for 1 - 3

+ Best Friend + Connection

+ Closest Relationship on Earth

+ Jesus + the Apostle John

LEVEL 3 - PERSONAL

+ Space for 3 - 9

+ Core Group + Accountability

+ Closest Group of Friends

+ Jesus + Three Disciples: Peter, James & John

LEVEL 4 - SOCIAL

+ Space for 9 - 25

+ Disciples + Community

+ Friends but also the Leadership Team

+ Jesus + Twelve Disciples

LEVEL 5 - PUBLIC

+ Space for 25+

+ People that love and are influenced by you

+ Have the least access to you

+ Jesus + Included 72 other disciples

No matter what space anyone may have in my life, they still have their OWN yard. They will always be responsible for all of their feelings, attitudes, and choices, as I will be responsible for all of mine. It's easy to immerse my yard with those who are closest to me. It will take significant obedience to God to stand in a place of ownership.

Knowing what I am responsible for, and what I am not, will only be half of the breakthrough I need to have. The other half will be putting it into practice in my daily life. **Knowing the truth is not enough; I will have to do the truth.**

Creating healthy relationships takes time and a consciousness of what belongs to whom. When we get this wrong, we can develop codependent relationships. We will believe we are responsible for things God did not ask us to manage.

"Codependency is a behavioral condition in a relationship where one person enables another person's addiction, poor mental health, immaturity, irresponsibility, or under-achievement. Among the core characteristics of codependency is an excessive reliance on other people for approval and a sense of identity." [1]

I can be in a relationship with someone behaving poorly and be desperate for them to change their behavior. I can get stuck believing that if I try hard enough, I can influence them to change.

Here's the HARD truth—**people who don't want to change, don't.**

When the wrong person wants them to change, they don't. No matter how much you want them to.

REAL CHANGE REQUIRES AN INWARD MOTIVATION.

When you accept that people only change when they want to change, life gets so much more manageable.

Most of the time we don't change without pain. Allowing others to experience the consequences of their actions isn't just a good idea, it's a God idea.

God created laws of boundaries and one of them is sowing and reaping.

1 Johnson, R. Skip (13 July 2014). "Codependency and Codependent Relationships". BPDFamily.com. Retrieved 9 September 2014.

AL

ANGE

QUIRES

INWAR

OTIVATIO

"Don't be misled: No one makes a fool of God. What a person plants, he will harvest. The person who plants selfishness, ignoring the needs of others—ignoring God!—harvests a crop of weeds. All he'll have to show for his life is weeds! But the one who plants in response to God, letting God's Spirit do the growth work in him, harvests a crop of real life, eternal life." Galatians 6:7

Likewise, we can become apathetic about our responsibilities, letting others take on more than God wants them to. Only when we respect each other's property lines will we have healthy, Godly, vibrant relationships.

REME MBER

+ The needs of others didn't dictate their exposure to Jesus while on Earth.

+ Relational spheres are places others have access to in my life.

+ I was not created to allow everybody into my inner world.

+ No matter what space anyone may have in my life, they still have their OWN yard.

+ People who don't want to change, don't. Real change requires an inward motivation.

+ Allowing others to experience the consequences of their actions isn't just a good idea, it's a God idea.

RELATIONSHIP Q & A

Q WHAT IF SOMEONE CONTINUES TO PUT THEIR FEELINGS, ATTITUDES, AND CHOICES IN MY YARD?

Irresponsible people love nothing more than for you to worry, be anxious, or feel responsible for their lives. **Your responsibility allows them to stay irresponsible.** So, reminding them that they own their yard is significant. (Note: just because you say it, doesn't mean they will change.) The point is for you to hear, believe, and act on your own words.

Repeatedly saying something like this will help:

"Since I can't control you, I've come to a decision..."

Once they understand this is your final answer, they will stop asking.

Q WHAT IF MY FRIEND IS ALWAYS TELLING ME THE SAME SAD STORY BUT NEVER TAKING MY ADVICE TO CHANGE IT?

A great way to place the responsibility back in their yard is to say something like,

"I think we've already been over this. I think when you are ready, you'll make a decision."

Instead of being annoyed, be prepared!

BY HAVILAH CUNNINGTON 179

Since you know they are going to ask you again, have your answer ready. Knowing your response will keep your anxiety down. When we are less anxious, we show up as the best version of ourselves.

Q **WHAT IF MY SPOUSE BELIEVES I'M RESPONSIBLE FOR THEIR HAPPINESS AND EACH TIME I CHALLENGE THEM ABOUT THEIR YARD, THEY BECOME ANGRY?**

Remember, their anger is about them. You cannot make anyone angry, including your spouse. Knowing this should help to ease your anxiety. One of the best tools I've learned is that I can't make someone respect my boundaries, but I can set standards.

Standards are an expectation of how I'm treated and what I will tolerate.

In a good **relationship**, I have **high expectations** for how I'm treated. I expect to be treated with kindness, love, affection, and respect. I do not tolerate emotional or physical abuse. I expect my partner to be loyal.

Communicating my standards sounds like:

"Because I love and respect you, I'm not willing to engage in disrespectful communication. So, when we can share respectfully with one another, I'll be happy to continue our discussion."

Or something like,

"It seems our communication is becoming disrespectful, (Don't say, "You are disrespectful!" Once accused, we often get defensive.) ... **I'm going to be in the**

other room, and would be happy to continue a healthy dialogue whenever we each want to do that."

The secret is to follow through with your standards so they believe you. Don't just threaten!

It's perfectly normal to ask for a time out to cool off.

Suppose you need to leave the conversation to think through your response. That is completely fine. Remember, responsible adults take care of themselves and know their limits.

The most important thing is to agree upon a return time to continue.

It would sound something like:

"This conversation isn't helping our relationship. So, I'm going to take a time out. I'd be happy to revisit this tomorrow, at 8AM, after my coffee."

Follow through without anger or punishment, and the next time you tell them you are leaving the room, they will believe you. They will quickly understand that if they want you there, they will need to change their behavior.

RESPOND

Let's take some time to understand where our relationships stand and make sure they are in the proper sphere.

You don't have to do this alone.

Start by putting God in the center of your life. Ask Him to help you design your relationships. Once you have this out in the open, you'll be able to create balance.

NOTE:

+ It's okay if some of your relationships are in the wrong sphere; they are each a work in progress. You are always allowed to change positions.

+ Relationships can be fluid and that's ok. Some relationships flourish during specific seasons, and for multiple reasons. Others will last a lifetime.

+ Sometimes you might even have a few blank spots. Studies show that we can only nurture about five to six intimate relationships at a time. Whew! Doesn't that make you feel better?

RELATIONAL SPHERES

Let's look at your current relationship spheres and how you want them to develop.

CURRENTLY
(Fill out with names)

LEVEL 1 - GOD SPOT

Is God in your God spot? Y/N

LEVEL 2 - INTIMATE

+

+

+

LEVEL 3 - PERSONAL

+	+
+	+
+	+

LEVEL 4 - SOCIAL

+	+
+	+
+	+
+	+
+	+

LEVEL 5 - PUBLIC

FUTURE

LEVEL 1 - GOD SPOT

LEVEL 2 - INTIMATE

+

+

+

LEVEL 3 - PERSONAL

+   +

+   +

+   +

LEVEL 4 - SOCIAL

+   +

+   +

+   +

+   +

+   +

LEVEL 5 - PUBLIC

HOW DO I PROTECT WHAT'S IMPORTANT TO ME?

I was driving home from taking the kids to school when God began speaking to me. I could hear His strong still voice on the inside of me.

He started, *"Havilah, things need to change in your life. You're presenting something to the world that isn't quite honest."*

I was confused. I asked Him to continue.

"From the outside looking in, you're presenting a life that seems to work effortlessly! The picture of you having it all and doing it all seems romantic, but there is much more to the equation behind the curtain. I've set you up for success."

He was right. The luxury of having a husband willing to work full-time to make this possible, and notably present grandparents, created the perfect chemistry. Each of their efforts allowed me to travel, speak, and write books for the past five years. I wasn't trying to hide it. I just didn't want to make others feel bad that I have this type of availability. But God began to speak to me about raising up a generation of women who could follow the call of God on their lives without neglecting their own families.

From the beginning of being in ministry, I knew I wanted to be home with my family. I had no interest in a nanny raising my kids. This zeal came from growing up in ministry environments where I met many ministry orphans and widows. Of course, this isn't an official title, but it really does define them — pastor kids and ministry wives were neglected for the sake of 'ministry.'

While growing up, a toxic way of thinking seemed to seep into the minds of Christian parents that sounded like, *"If I serve God, God will take care of my family"* or *"If I give my life to the ministry, God will raise my kids for me."*

Sounds spiritual, right? After all, doesn't God give us grace as a family?

Yes, but...

GOD ALSO CREATED US TO BE POWERFUL IN EVERY SPHERE OF OUR LIVES.

Passing our stewardship off to other people with the hope that *"God will clean it up if we mess it up,"* isn't accurate or spiritual.

I'll never forget hearing this, **"Havilah, when Jesus said, 'Go into all the world,' He was saying to you, 'Havilah, go into your living room!'"**

I had never thought of it like this!

It was like a punch to my spiritual gut.

"Wait a minute - so for me to fulfill the call of God on my life, I'm allowed to say "No!" to the crowd so that I can serve my little congregation of four?" I was asking God this question for real.

To which He replied, **"Absolutely!"**

I could feel a profound relief wash over me. Serving God, in the most intimate relationships in my life, was pleasing to Him. Wow!

Ministry people seem to be the worst at this. We go into a life of service for the right reasons. We want to lay our lives down for the call, picking up our cross, and following Jesus.

But at what cost?

Statistics are clear. Our decision to "forsake all" often means abandoning our closest relationships. We are slapping an "I'm too busy for God to take time for my family" sticker on our spiritual shirts. Sure, serving our kids is anything but glamorous, but perhaps Jesus knew this when He said in **Matthew 5:3, "Blessed are the poor in spirit for theirs is the kingdom of heaven"** or in verse 5, **"You're blessed when you're content with just who you are—no more, no less. That's the moment you find yourselves proud owners of everything that can't be bought." Matthew 5:5 (MSG)**

Of course, there's the other side of the coin.

Some of us have entirely lost ourselves in our child's life, living vicariously through them and forgetting who we were before our stewardship of parenthood.

God challenged me the day I sat in my car. He said,

"I want you to live a life that is duplicatable. I want you to show the world that being a wife isn't a burden and that you don't have to neglect your family to follow me."

To unpack this, we'll need to define our priorities. Let's start by understanding how to set our priorities without feeling bad about them.

LET'S START BY UNDERSTANDING HOW TO SET OUR PRIORITIES WITHOUT FEELING BAD ABOUT THEM.

5 STEPS TO DISCOVERING YOUR PRIORITIES

(Use the space to write your thoughts but consider grabbing a journal for more room to write freely!)

ONE // ENVISION YOUR BEST LIFE

What would your best life look like? What would it look like to live an abundant life? Take some time to write freely. Reflect on what your best life would look like regarding time, faith, family, marriage, money, physical health, friendships, work, home, etc. How can you live worthy of the calling to which you have been called?

(Write your thoughts)

_____

_____

_____

_____

Jesus said, "I came that they may have and enjoy life, and have it in abundance [to the full, till it overflows]."
John 10:10 (AMP)

When you look back at the end of your life, what do you want to be known for or how would you want to be remembered?

_____

_____

_____

"So I, the prisoner for the Lord, appeal to you to live a life worthy of the calling to which you have been called [that is, to live a life that exhibits godly character, moral courage, personal integrity, and mature behavior—a life that expresses gratitude to God for your salvation]..."
Ephesians 4:1 (AMP)

TWO // IDENTIFY WHAT'S WORKING AND WHAT ISN'T WORKING

Take a look at your current life. First, make a list of what is working. Write down the things you are doing right.

_____

_____

_____

_____

If you had no other obligations, how would you spend your time?

_____

_____

_____

_____

List all of the things that are not working.
What are your biggest distractions?

_____

_____

_____

What leaves you feeling frustrated, cranky, and defeated at the end of the day?

What keeps you from spending time on the things that bring you joy?

THREE // CHOOSE YOUR TOP FIVE

Now let's dig deep and identify the five most important things in your life.

What are your core desires? What are the things that fuel your soul and make you want to get out of bed in the morning?

What are the things that will cause you the most regret at the end of your life, if you do not take the time to focus on them now?

_____

_____

_____

_____

List the TOP FIVE areas of your life that you would most love to devote your time to above all else.

1.

2.

3.

4.

5.

These are your priorities.

FOUR // EVALUATE YOUR SCHEDULE

Take a good, hard look at the things that are taking up your time.

If someone from the outside listed your priorities based on how you spend your time, would they come to the same conclusion you did?

_____

_____

_____

_____

Does your schedule reflect the things that are most important to you?

_____

_____

_____

FIVE // LEARN TO SAY NO

You will have to say "No!" to good things in order to say "Yes!" to great things.

How you spend your time will vary from season to season. What do you need to say "No!" to right now so you can say "Yes!" in the future? (Write your thoughts)

_____

_____

_____

_____

_____

_____

Now you get to structure your YARD to maintain these important things in your life.

REME MBER

+ God does not ask me to forsake my most important and intimate relationships for the sake of ministry.

+ God created me to be powerful in every sphere of my life.

+ Passing my stewardship off to other people in hopes that *"God will clean it up if we mess it up,"* isn't accurate or spiritual.

+ We need to define our priorities.

+ My priorities will confirm my Kingdom-filter.

But first and most importantly seek (aim at, strive after) His kingdom and His righteousness [His way of doing and being right—the attitude and character of God], and all these things will be given to you also. Matthew 6:33 (AMP)

"Seeking His Kingdom" isn't just another thing for me to fit on my list of priorities – or to put at the top. Instead, it's the filter in which I do everything. I seek first the Kingdom of God.

I will rarely have to choose between honoring God and loving my spouse and children or being a good worker. I glorify God and seek first the Kingdom of God by being a good spouse, mother, and a good worker.

When I first gave my life to Christ, the primary choice I made was to seek His Kingdom. Every day, my life will either reinforce that decision or deny it.

My priorities will confirm my Kingdom-filter.

BY HAVILAH CUNNINGTON 197

RESPOND

MIND MAPPING

Today, we're going to practice *Mind Mapping.*
(See example below)

Mind Maps are diagrams where we put our thinking into visual
pictures, symbols, numbers, and words. These "maps" are
based on the configuration of a brain cell.

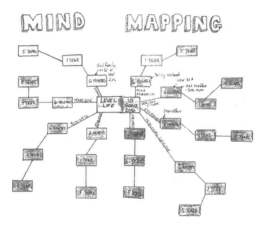

Like a brain cell, mind maps have a core with dendrites (lines)
shooting out from the center. The "lines" include images, words,
or numbers.

*Research says our brains don't work up and down or linear—
they work circular—around and around—thus helping us see the
relationships, associations, and connections of how the pieces
connect to the whole.*

Mind mapping is a very spontaneous way of thinking and an
essential component of creative thinking.

Let's get started:

1. By hand, draw a circle in the middle of a piece of paper.

2. Draw six lines extending from the circle. The lines touch the main circle.

3. In the center circle, write the primary purpose/priority in your life. If you are thinking visually and want images or symbols along with the words—include them.

4. On each of the six extended lines, write or draw images of various aspects or goals you are working on.

5. You can also have lines that branch out from each line—with words or images about each issue.

6. Make your map colorful—use at least three colors.

7. Use keywords and write in all upper-case or lower-case letters.

8. Develop your own particular style of mind-mapping. Make it represent YOU!

I DO BOUNDARIES

FINAL THOUGHTS

It's been an incredible journey together!

I hope you've had a chance to discover that Godly, breathable boundaries are absolutely possible. You can live an abundant life without anyone else participating. Praise God!

Remember, knowing how God designed you and choosing to only carry your load is the best way to protect what matters most to you.

My hope for you is that you will communicate your boundaries with confidence. It will take time and diligence but it is entirely possible. Practice. Practice. Practice.

My dream is that you will teach those around you these life-changing skills...so that no one grows up believing God has to abuse them to use them.

Remember to return those heavy backpacks to their rightful owners with kindness, honesty, and conviction. You can do this!

Much Love & Grace

Lavilah

RESOURCES & NEXT STEPS

BOOKS

I Do Hard Things

Taken from the story of Joseph, the man who conquered the unthinkable in his own life and learned to see God's purpose in his painful path. This study is designed for those who are passionately obsessed with learning how to live their life the way God intended. If you are no longer willing to settle for a life of debilitating shame and crippling fear, if you are convinced there's more, then this study is for you!

Eat, Pray, Hustle

Eat, Pray, Hustle is a four-week study designed to help you understand the attributes of a God Dream. We will journey through the story of Abraham and unpack what it looks like to go after our dreams with God. Dream chasing is a huge part of life with God. We were never meant to watch from the sidelines; we were always meant to be part of the story.

RESOURCES TO GROW EVERY DAY

ONLINE COURSES

Spiritual Development
Discover your gifts and steward your calling

✴ Prophetic Personalities
✴ Purpose
✴ Parenting Sexuality
✴ Moms Of Men

Video Bible Studies
Guided studies to grow you in God's Word

✴ I Do Hard Things
✴ Leap Into Love
✴ Eat, Pray, Hustle
✴ Soul Food
✴ Radical Growth
✴ The Good Stuff

Grow Your Influence
Crash courses to communication

✴ Writing A Book
✴ Delivering A Message
✴ Message Prep
✴ Going Live Simplified

Find all these books, courses and more at
shop.truthtotable.com

TRUTH ACADEMY

YOUR PATHWAY TO EVERYDAY SPIRITUAL GROWTH

Mentoring, Curriculum + Community inside Truth to Table

AT A GLANCE

- More than 200 video lessons + new lessons added regularly
- Downloadable study guides and full length E-books
- A supportive online community
- Exclusive discounts
- VIP customer support

INCLUDED IN MEMBERSHIP

Core Bible Studies

All E-Courses

Live Q&A's

Master Classes

Guest Content

Full-Length Messages

LEARN MORE
& JOIN TODAY

truthtotable.com/academy

"Truth to Table is an authentic community of people wanting to grow in Christ and do life well in their God journey."

LAURA ANSLOW
TRUTH TO TABLE MEMBER

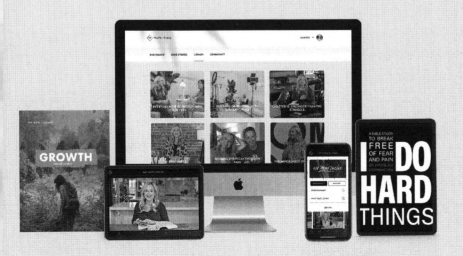

STAY CONNECTED

 **Website & Newsletter**
TRUTHTOTABLE.COM

 **Instagram**
@TRUTHTOTABLE

 **Facebook**
/TRUTHTOTABLE

 **Podcast**
HAVILAHCUNNINGTON.COM/PODCAST-FEED

 **Email**
INFO@TRUTHTOTABLE.COM

SPIRITUAL GROWTH THROUGH EVERYDAY WINS

FREE RESOURCES FOR GROWTH

Text **GROW** to **833.593.0218** to join **FREE!**

IT'S FREE

START YOUR GUIDED GROWTH EXPERIENCE TODAY!

REQUEST AN EVENT

Havilah would love to consider joining you for your next event. Here are a few types of events she's successfully partnered with.

- Women's Events
- Conferences
- Weekend Services
- Workshops & More

For event inquiries or any other questions contact info@truthtotable.com

SUPPORT THE MOVEMENT

GET THE LATEST NEWS

Stay connected and updated on all the latest content, resources, events dates and more — Sign up for our newsletter!

PRAY

We value and appreciate your prayers as we work to empower as many people as possible to grow a vibrant life in God.

DONATE

Consider supporting some of our upcoming projects with a financial donation. We are a non-profit.

Current projects include: translation of all of our resources and mobile app development.

*Truth To Table is a 501c3 non-proft

NOTES

I DO BOUNDARIES

I DO BOUNDARIES

Manufactured by Amazon.ca
Bolton, ON

18657001R00120